God Here and Now

"This volume brings together essays and addresses from the period of Barth's greatest maturity and breadth as a Christian theologian. Together they constitute some of Barth's best shorter work: rooted in prodigious knowledge of and love for the faith of the church, they are calm, concentrated statements of the Christian gospel as it addresses both the church and the world. Here in brief compass we can see Barth the dogmatician, Barth the ecumenist and Barth the Christian humanist allowing the gospel's wisdom to address central issues of Christian faith, action and witness in the world."

Professor John Webster, Oxford University

"Karl Barth was a man of his time. Yet he was also a genius, able to see a little further than many and to offer new insights into the ways of God and mankind."

Professor Colin Gunton, The Times

"With a startling suddenness [Barth's] message has transformed the whole outlook of Protestant theology on the continent."

The Times Literary Supplement

Karl
Barth

God Here and Now

Translated by Paul M. van Buren
With a new introduction by George Hunsinger

London and New York

This book is a compilation of the following German texts: *Die Aktualitat der christlichen Botschaft* 1949/50; *Die Souveranitat des Wortes Gottes und die Engscheidung des Glaubens* 1939; *Die Botschaft von der freien Gnade Gottes* 1947; *Die Autoritat und Bedeutung der Bibel* 1947; *Die Kirche – die lebendige Gemeinde des lebendigen Herrn Jesus Christus* 1947; *Christliche Ethik* 1946; *Humanismus* 1950

English edition first published in United Kingdom 1964
by Routledge & Kegan Paul

First published in Routledge Classics 2003
by Routledge
11 New Fetter Lane, London EC4P 4EE
29 West 35th Street, New York, NY 10001

Routledge is an imprint of the Taylor & Francis Group

German original version © 1964, 2003 Theologischer Verlag Zürich

Introduction to Routledge Classics edition © 2003 George Hunsinger

Typeset in Joanna by RefineCatch Limited, Bungay, Suffolk
Printed and bound in Great Britain by
TJ International Ltd, Padstow, Cornwall

British Library Cataloguing in Publication Data
A catalogue record for this book is available from the British Library

Library of Congress Cataloging in Publication Data
A catalog record for this book has been requested

ISBN 0–415–30447–4

Contents

INTRODUCTION TO THE ROUTLEDGE CLASSICS EDITION

It is almost always better to read Karl Barth than to read about him. He has a wonderful way of dispelling any caricatures that may have arisen at second hand. The essays collected in this volume are among his finest shorter writings. For those just starting out with Barth, they are an excellent place to begin. They are like foothills from which one might wish eventually to scale the lofty heights of his great work, Church Dogmatics. His theology at lower altitude is less demanding and more accessible. Yet it remains as bold, confident and provocative as in the higher reaches of his work.

Dietrich Bonhoeffer once suggested that in Barth we find the same hilaritas as we do in Mozart. The good cheer which knows how to incorporate all that is negative within itself yet without losing its basic gladness is surely one of Barth's most appealing characteristics. It is a hilaritas informed by gravitas, but which never succumbs to it. For all his greatness, or perhaps just because of it, Barth does not take himself too seriously. Along with *hilaritas* and *gravitas*, an element of *humilitas* pervades his work. Barth has no higher aspiration than to place his intellect in the service of God's grace. Grace inspires the cheerfulness, the gravity and the humility that he sees as proper to the theologian's task.

A crucial distinction recurs in these essays between abstract system and concrete history. Barth considers a viewpoint to be "abstract" if it mistakes the part for the whole. An abstraction is a kind of misplaced concreteness. It takes something that is necessary but not sufficient and treats it as though it were both. Although it is wrong to assign sufficiency to a view that lacks it, Barth almost never describes such a viewpoint as "false." He is more inclined to call it "abstract." It contains elements of truth configured into an improper whole.

Concreteness depends on ascribing centrality to Jesus Christ. He is the fulfillment of all the ways of God with humankind. In him revelation and salvation are one. According to Barth, Jesus Christ is primarily his life-history. His being is in his life-history even as his person is in his work. The Incarnation is the history of Jesus Christ as fulfilled in his atoning death and revealed in his resurrection from the dead. No system can account for the occurrence of this extraordinary history. It is either taken on its own terms, as attested by Holy Scripture, or not at all.

Theological concepts, metaphors and viewpoints that respect the significance of this history are not abstract but concrete. They are necessarily descriptive rather than explanatory, because what they are attesting—the mystery of the Incarnation—is unique in kind. Moreover, if they are to be concrete, they can never aspire to the kind of closure—the unity and totality—that Barth associates with a system. They are concrete precisely by remaining open-textured in their orientation to the mystery of Christ. They point to a reality that can never be mastered by concepts, but which necessarily masters them.

The Incarnation—the history of Jesus Christ—as understood by Barth is not a system, nor does it compete with any system. Theology necessarily subjects all "systems" or "worldviews" (whether overt or covert) to critical appraisal and dissolution, affirming what is valid, discarding what is not. It thereby orders all ideas, as far as possible, into a proper relation to Christ at the center, and just so to one another. There is no reason why theology might not learn a great deal from any worldview in the process, and every reason to expect that it would. Nor is there any reason for theology to set itself up as a kind of supersystem in which all questions can be arbitrated and resolved. Many questions remain beyond theology's ken. In that sense Barth would reject the slogan that "scripture absorbs the world." A modest revision—that by attesting the centrality of Christ, scripture reorients the world—would be more in the spirit of his thought.

In Chapter 1 Barth interprets the Incarnation as the humanism of God. This move illustrates the method of critical assimilation. Rather than subjecting theology to any form of humanism, Barth reconfigures humanism by subjecting it to Christ. God's humanism, the Incarnation, is "an event which has happened *once and for all time*" (p. 5). It is a particular, unrepeatable event, yet with universal significance. What it means for human beings to be human and what it means for God to be God are revealed by the particular human being, Jesus Christ (p. 6).

The centrality of Christ does not invalidate other forms of

human self-understanding. "The assertions of man's under-standing of himself need not thereby be ruled out as false" (pp. 6–7). After a quick survey of humanisms, Barth states:

> In the light of the Christian proclamation, that may all be true, but it is true only if it comprehends, is subordinated to, and understood in connection with [. . . Jesus Christ . . .], man exists from God and for God, and as God's creature is rushing toward Him and His eternal life.
>
> (p. 7)

The centrality of Christ would affirm, and not exclude, any actually existing secular truth. "That is the basis on which the Christian proclamation may make peace with classical and every other humanism, though it might also be the cause of conflict with them" (p. 7).

The opening section of Chapter 2 offers a glimpse of how *hilaritas* might incorporate *gravitas* without succumbing to it. The "god of this world," who generates fear and wreaks havoc, is described soberly and in perplexity yet without despair. What-ever the appearances to the contrary, the God of Abraham, Isaac and Jacob and the Father of our Lord Jesus Christ can and does, Barth believes, take care of himself—and at the same time also of us. Every obligation we might supposedly have toward this world's god is dissolved by the cross of Christ. "Every (really every!) anxiety which we could have in this world was removed in Him. He, Jesus Christ, stands as Victor over our sins of yesterday, today, and tomorrow, over the hosts of tempta-tion, over the horror of death and hell" (p. 19). It remains for us to live a life of gratitude in service to the triumph of grace.

Gratitude to Christ will not be uncritical of alien views. Other words may harmonize with God's Word, but God's

Word does not harmonize with them. "For there exists no second and third, but only one Word of God" (p. 22). God's Word, states Barth, can therefore "be heard only exclusively, or else not at all. Other words can be only its echo or a response to it, giving a contradictory or acknowledging answer. As God is unique, so is His Word" (p. 22). Solidarity with the world for which Christ died must be enacted, paradoxically, in solitary witness to exclusive truth. There is no solidarity without this witness, and no exclusive truth without this solidarity.

"God Himself . . . is free grace" (p. 35), writes Barth, setting forth the theme of Chapter 3. Grace represents the "objective, ontological circumstance" in which we live out our lives (p. 39). Grace is free and sovereign. It is free to remain with the church despite all the church's obvious and hidden imperfections (p. 53). It is free also to operate outside the church in incognito ways. "We must reckon with the fact that it can always be at work outside the walls of the Church and can be announced even by quite other tongues than those that have been given to us" (p. 43). What the ultimate scope of grace will be we cannot say. "Strange Christianity, whose most pressing anxiety seems to be that God's grace might prove to be all too free on this side, that hell, instead of being populated with so many people, might some day prove to be empty!" (p. 42).

There is a humilitas involved when faith acknowledges the limitations of what it can know. We do not know, for example, how grace will take shape in its final revelation of exclusion and embrace. It is better not to speculate too closely.

For we do not know what will be revealed when the last covering is removed from our eyes, from all eyes: how we shall behold one another and what we shall be to one another—men of today and men of past centuries and millennia, ancestors and descendants, husbands and wives, wise and foolish, oppressors and oppressed, traitors and betrayed, murderers and murdered, West and East, Germans and others, Christians, Jews, and heathen, orthodox and heretics, Catholics and Protestants, Lutheran and Reformed; upon what divisions and unions, what confrontations and cross-connections the seals of all books will be opened; how much will seem small and unimportant to us then, how much will only then appear great and important; for what surprises of all kinds we must prepare ourselves.

(pp. 45–6)

We know only one thing: that Christ is the same, yesterday, today and forever, "that His grace is whole and complete," that it endures "through time into eternity," and that one day it will "exist and be recognized in a totally different way" than it is now (p. 46).

On the authority and significance of the Bible, the theme of Chapter 4, the argument turns largely on Barth's use of the term "form." By saying that the Bible is the objective form of Christ's presence and lordship here and now, Barth is ascribing sacramental status to the scriptures. The Bible functions, in effect, as the real presence of the Lord Jesus Christ. Christ the incarnate Word is present in, with and under the written word of the scriptures. Two main ideas seem to be at stake here: mediation and witness.

Mediation involves the real presence of Christ here and now, while witness involves his saving accomplishment there and then. Although the scriptures function both to mediate

Jesus Christ and attest him, it is the concept of witness which receives the primacy. That is because, with Luther and the Reformation, Barth believes that the decisive locus of salvation is to be found in what Christ has accomplished apart from us (*extra nos*)—in his life-history as fulfilled in his death. "On Golgotha," he writes, "*everything* was accomplished" (p. 19).

Scripture is the normative witness to that accomplishment. In Christ—in his life-history, in his incarnate person as found in his work, and in his saving work as bound to his person—we have been reconciled to God and made heirs of eternal life. In its witnessing function, therefore, Scripture points away from the present and back to what has been done for us on the Cross once for all. Witness is the controlling idea in Barth's understanding of Scripture, because the "perfect tense" takes precedence over the "present tense."

Witness gives us the identity of Jesus Christ, and mediation gives us his presence. He is present to us here and now, by virtue of his Resurrection, as the one who has accomplished our salvation there and then. The scriptures that attest him in his saving identity also mediate him in his saving presence. It is he himself, not the church, who is Lord of this event. He himself sees to it that he is acknowledged for who he is through the church's faithful proclamation. He himself sees to it that the word of the prophets and the apostles functions in the community in this witnessing and mediating way.

The function of Scripture in witness and mediation, according to Barth, is best understood as "non-foundational." It is something that is "purely given" (p. 56). It occurs as an ongoing event that is grounded in nothing other than itself. It is a high miracle occurring through the high mystery of the real presence of Christ the Lord.

The essence of the church, the theme of Chapter 5, is best described, Barth suggests, as a history (p. 83). The church is a "dynamic reality" arising from Christ's resurrection and hastening toward his future self-revelation (p. 76). It is essentially a happening that occurs "between the times." It occurs as a community of remembrance, vocation and hope. It attests the reconciliation in Christ that has already taken place, and awaits the ultimate unity of all things to eternal life. In its vocation of attesting Christ, it is a living community—"the living congregation of the living Lord Jesus Christ" (p. 75).

This community is constituted, as Barth sees it, by the proclamation of the gospel. When the centrality of the Word is acknowledged, then the essence of the church can be expressed in any number of different ways. The church's essence is a matter not only of witness but also of fellowship, not only of proclamation but also of sacrament, not only of being endangered but also of being preserved. In every aspect, however, it is always primarily a question of the Word. "It is a question of the congregation being ready, open, and free for God's Word and for the renewal of the Church by God's Word" (p. 101). The Christ who operates through the Word is the hope, comfort and renewal of the church. "The hope and the only hope of the Church is that He so speak His Word that the corresponding answer is found among Christians, that He accept and and make use of the witness of His apostles once again, that He make the exposition and application of this witness strong, deep, and contemporary in laying hold of men" (p. 93). Just so is the church's essence a history.

Christian ethics, as explained in Chapter 6, is a matter of work and prayer (p. 113). It involves the work that begins in prayer, and the prayer that ends in work. It calls continually upon God even as it seeks to live in accord with its petitions, thanks and praise. Its ethics is an answer to the call and command of God. The primary acting subject who must always be taken into account is not the human being but God. "God does something and does it in such a way that man is thereby called to do something in turn" (p. 107). The call of God, as it goes forth in the history between God and all who know him in love by faith, is God's command. Human conduct is therefore good when it corresponds to the indicative of God's grace (p. 109). What God has graciously done for us includes the divine imperative within itself.

In the final chapter on "humanism," Barth reflects on the ten-day conference that he had attended with other European intellectuals and where he had presented what is now the first chapter in this collection. After summarizing what some of his secular colleagues had said in their lectures, he finds himself wondering whether the real human being, the contemporary human being, had come into the picture at all. "The problem of guilt was not so much as touched on in those ten days," he ponders, "and the problem of death was only barely touched" (p. 127). Moreover, how could the real human being be seen "where no one could speak out of a genuine, comforting certainty and hope?" (p. 127).

What it means to be human is not available concretely if the total relevant context is not taken into account, and that means taking into account human existence as determined by the centrality of Christ. It means taking human existence into account as defined by his judgment and grace.

> How can we speak constructively about what is meant by the label "humanism," about real contemporary man and his future if we do not know and do not *want* to know that man is in fact lost and also in fact saved, if one does not know

and does not want to know the true horror and the true hope of our situation? The true man for all time is the lost and rescued man who is seen in the mirror of Jesus Christ.

(p. 128)

Only through Jesus Christ can what it means to be human be seen in the full depth of its misery and the full dignity of its hope.

In conclusion, it would be best not to mistake what Barth means when he compares the mission of the church to the task of being a letter carrier (p. 49). The church is commissioned to deliver a message not of its own devising and whose contents are not at its discretion. It is the message of the gracious mystery of the Incarnation. The grace of this mystery is sheer gift even as the mystery of this grace is better met with adoration than with grudging consternation.

While the content of this message is fixed, the mode of its presentation is a matter of keen responsibility. The church must not only place itself in the service of this message. It must do so with all "its own power, faith, [and] skill" (p. 49). Proclamation is a task requiring Christians who are "nimble, humble, questioning, seeking, asking, knocking" (p. 53). When we cease to be such persons and fall asleep, grace will rouse us like a trumpet blast from our slumbers (p. 53). We will then know anew that we are called to proclaim the mystery of Incarnation with all the intelligence, boldness, taste and good cheer that we can muster. But then we will also know that the outcome lies beyond our control, for "it is His decision, the decision of the Word of God, just when and where our choice is the choice of truth in adoration" (p. 23).

GEORGE HUNSINGER

TRANSLATOR'S INTRODUCTION

The seven addresses here translated were originally delivered within the past fifteen years by the Swiss theologian Karl Barth before such diverse audiences as the Amsterdam Assembly of the World Council of Churches and a select gathering of secular European intellectuals. The selection and arrangement of the material by the author and the editor of this volume are designed to give a fair presentation of Barth's mature thought. I have done my best to reproduce something of his personal style as well as the content of his thought in English, but I am left with the conviction that the major task of translating Barth for Americans must finally be accomplished by each reader for himself. American readers may be helped to appreciate both the power and the problem of Barth's theology, however, by an introduction from one American who studied for three years with Barth, who followed loyally in his teacher's steps for some time, but who has found the Barthian path increasingly difficult to discern in the American scene.

Barth deserves the attention of anyone interested in Christian thought in our century. He is the most influential theologian since Schleiermacher, and more than any other man he has revitalized and set the terms for Protestant theology since the end of the First World War. Protestants will only rightly assess Barth, however, when they take note of the fact that for some years he has been attracting increasing attention from Roman Catholic theologians, and it is at least conceivable that Barth's thinking may eventually find among Catholics its most fertile soil. Catholics as well as Protestants have noticed in Barth a man in intimate conversation with a long past, especially with the past of the sixteenth century, but reaching back also to the medieval School-men and the ancient Greek and Latin Fathers, and including above all others the biblical authors. Americans may feel that Barth is a man for whom the turning point in theology and thought lies in the first half of the sixteenth century, rather than in the second half of the eighteenth century, where we might be more inclined to locate it. Yet if we would learn something of what it is like to be a man of the twentieth century in intimate conversation with the long past of theology (and thereby perhaps learn something more of that past than is easily discernable from these New World shores) it will be worth our while never to dismiss this man as a relic of an antique world or as a conservative or reactionary who will not move with the times. He may even help us to overcome what some might call our myopia sufficiently to enable us to notice that there have been other men of faith before us who have wrestled with many problems which we face. He may even help us to be helped by them. At the least, we may be shown something of the glory of the ancient tradition of the apostles and martyrs and Fathers, filtered through the Reformers of the sixteenth century, and commented on and presented to us by a brilliant contemporary traditionalist.

Barth, as these essays make plain, is a theologian's theologian. His *Church Dogmatics* is of course a gold mine for theologians, a veritable encyclopedia of theological reflection from all ages, skillfully and profoundly expounded by an able man. But primarily, Barth stands as a theologian in the service of preaching. Preaching, as he conceives it, is an activity which takes place between the biblical texts and their faithful hearer. Time does not affect this picture; Barth seems to conceive of the preacher as a man without dates in history who is seeking to hear just what the biblical texts said of old, and who, having heard, stands up to pass on precisely what he has heard. This faithful listener who has become the preacher is only a mailman, Barth says, delivering a letter which he has neither written nor altered. He is an amateur trumpeter, and no matter how unskilled he may be, his trumpet will awaken the sleepers.

There is an indubitable power here just because Barth refuses to ask about the mailman's ability to read the letter to an illiterate recipient or to translate it into the native language. He likewise refuses to ask more than that we let the trumpet sound its own note, regardless of what tune we might like to hear or play. He refuses to consider the questions of *how* men use and understand language and whether this changes with time and situation, and consequently he is able to concentrate on *what* is said to men in the gospel. The result is not only a sure voice that never quavers with doubt; it is one which has at its command all the wealth of past ages of assurance. In no small measure because of this refusal to stand between us and the past with which he is in conversation, Barth's theology is powerful.

As Americans listen to him in this conversation—and a brilliant conversationalist is always a joy to hear—they will be tempted to be typically themselves and ask, But is he in conversation with *us*? By refusing to consider the way we use words today and the categories with which we think, has he not shut us out of his conversation? What are we to make of the metaphor of the trumpet? It may surely wake men, but will it wake them to attack or to retreat? Is it not more likely still that they will simply groan and roll over at the strange noise of uneven, meaningless notes? These peculiar metaphors and the questions which they raise in us reveal both the power and also the problem of Barth as a guide for contemporary American Christians. Only history can tell whether Barth's thought will prove powerful and helpful in America. The problem lies in his neat separation of the *how* of language from the *what*. Can a word, whether called human or divine, really be considered as a package which bears its own meaning wrapped inside it? Are the analogies of a letter carried by a mailman or a trumpet blown by a novice really to the point? Whatever our doubts, Barth stands before us in the posture of one stuffing a letter into our mailbox or blowing a blast on the trumpet. Certainly we can at the very least learn from him what it was that postmen in earlier ages were delivering to people on their mail routes, and this is surely part of what we should appropriate if we would understand the heart of the matter with which both Barth and American theologians are concerned. Each reader will have to decide for himself if the message comes through to him in such a way that he can make it his own. It may be added that it has been the puzzling experience of some who would claim that this has happened to them, thanks to this particular Swiss mailman, that the mailman has not been too pleased when they have seriously tried to understand the message in their peculiar American way. Be that as it may, let us turn now to the letter the mailman would deliver.

God Here and Now, really *God* and really *here and now*: that is what Barth has to say; that is the trumpet call. The other way in which he says this is simply: the name Jesus Christ. That one man in the midst of all other men is all that matters, and so the proclamation of this man as the form and content of *God Here and Now* is Barth's only concern. In the first chapter Barth is speaking to contemporary humanists of every conceivable persuasion. He is completely himself, with his foundation firm and clear. He does not hesitate, therefore, to meet his hearers this far: the message of the gospel may also be called a sort of humanism, but one which arises out of the acknowledgment that God's "here and now" in the person of the man Jesus defines every man in his "here and now." The faithful hearer of the biblical message, as Barth sees it, has no right to enter into any discussion of man in general. He can speak only on the basis of one particular man, and if that man is proclaimed, Barth concludes, he will prove his own point.

Just as Barth does not feel qualified to talk about man in general when he speaks as a theologian, so in the second chapter he makes the corollary point that faith knows nothing about God in general, but only about the God who has made himself "here and now" in Jesus of Nazareth. Language about God becomes adequate and proper, not as it is adjusted to this world or to the understanding of the listener, but only as it takes the form of speaking of Christ, and of the decision of faith which characterized his history and which stands as a claim over every man, a claim which calls for a response as concrete and as involved in life as was Jesus of Nazareth himself.

Whether he starts from a question about man or a question about God, then, Barth offers us only one place in which to look, where all this has become concrete: Jesus Christ, proclaimed as the definition and reality of both God and man, "here and now." This is all that the Church has to say, this message of God's free grace which is the message concerning Jesus Christ. If Barth at one point can say that care must be exercised by the Church in presenting this message in the language understood by the people, this consists, so he maintains, in letting the biblical message speak what it wants to say, even word for word. Proclamation is only this delivery of the biblical message.

Perhaps it will be somewhere in the chapter on this proclamation, or in the following chapter on the Bible (on which Barth claims to base the proclamation), that American Christians will find it hardest to follow Barth and his particular conception of how to read and understand the biblical writings. He stands before our amazed eyes as a sort of Luther *redivivus*, refusing to allow any weight to the fact that anything important, at least anything which the Christian should regard as important, has happened to our world with the coming of science, industrialization, technology, and the consequent revolution in our way of thinking. As can be seen in his *Protestant Thought from Rousseau to Ritschl*, Barth has indeed noticed this revolution, but he would turn us away from it with a solemn "nevertheless" and take us back to what we were speaking of before all that happened, urging us to continue that earlier conversation and carry it further.

Jesus Christ, witnessed to in Scripture, proclaimed out of faithful listening to that witness—that is *God here and now*; and there the Church comes in, as the congregation assembled to hear that proclamation. Insofar as it hears and acknowledges it, insofar as it is truly a matter of God becoming "here and now" for that congregation, there is the Church, be it in the local parish or in some other form of gathering together, as in the ecumenical movement. If that Church becomes sick and weak or in danger of the death of turning into a religious club and becoming no longer the Church, then there is only one remedy: that it be reborn and renewed by being spoken to once more by the living word concerning the living Jesus Christ, and by responding to this.

The response can only be one of thanksgiving, and around this theme Barth builds the basis of his ethics: since man's true existence lies in responding to God here and now, and since God here and now is Jesus Christ, Christian ethics can define the good only as being thankful for grace, nothing more nor less. But because grace has been made concrete, so the ethics of thankfulness is and must be just as concrete, just as vitally concerned with and involved in this world.

Barth concludes this summary of his thought by reflecting on the course of the meeting at which he delivered the address which forms Chapter 1. This conclusion should be particularly helpful to Americans trying to understand him and possibly tempted to say that his is a voice from another world and another age. In this last chapter, Barth shows how deeply he is concerned about man and about men, how earnestly he wishes that men could have the one thing that is needful in order that this world might be somehow a better world. And he closes as he begins by offering simply and humbly the one needful thing as he has seen it: Jesus of Nazareth. That for which the world longs and which it pursues with all its philosophies and metaphysics, with its -isms and ideologies, is to be found in him to whom theology points with its language about true God and true man.

PAUL M. VAN BUREN
AUSTIN, TEXAS

1

THE CHRISTIAN PROCLAMATION HERE AND NOW[1]

In these days, intellectuals of widely different backgrounds and interests are concerned with the subject of a "new humanism." Two theologians have been asked to address themselves to the question of the relevance of the Christian proclamation, the Christian proclamation here and now, the Rev. P. Maydieu for Catholic theology and I for Protestant theology.

This situation is hardly self-explanatory. Forty or fifty years ago, no one would have so much as thought of inviting

---

[1] An address delivered before the *Rencontres Internationales* held in Geneva, Switzerland, in 1949 on the subject, "A New Humanism." Barth and a Catholic theologian were the only Christians in this conference of Western European intellectuals. Ed.

theologians to participate in such a discussion. Perhaps a representative of the field of so-called Philosophy of Religion might have been acceptable, but surely not a theologian taking his stand upon the faith of his Church. I leave open the question how it is that we find ourselves in this situation which would have been impossible then, but I would call to your attention that our participation implies a certain risk.

Why should we theologians not be open to all the different perspectives from which our subject, a new humanism, is to be developed and discussed in these days? We will, of course, have to stick to our business, namely, the business of the Christian Church. Or more precisely, we will have to stick to that to which the Christian Church owes its existence and which it wishes to serve. Surely we will not be expected by the other participants in this discussion to be ashamed of theology. I am sure we will be granted the benefit of *sint ut sunt aut non sint*. But it is just at this point that they begin to run a certain risk. If the Christian proclamation is announced in its fullness, being neither hidden nor diluted, and if it is to be spoken of as something "here and now," as indeed it must be if it is to be properly spoken of, this might possibly cause embarrassment or even distress. Neither the Catholic nor the Protestant theologian will be able to conceal the fact that the Christian proclamation would be misunderstood today, as it always has been, if it were presented as one among many theoretical, moral, or aesthetic principles or systems, as one "ism" in competition, harmony, or conflict with other "isms." Nor will we be able to conceal the fact that today as always, in the face of all men and all human opinions and strivings, the Christian proclamation intends to make known God's will, work, and revelation. We shall also not be able to hide the fact that in the Christian proclamation, it is a

2

question neither of a classical humanism nor of a new one to be discovered today, but of God's humanism. We shall further not be able to hide the fact that this humanism of God's, on the one hand, exists and can be comprehended only in a quite specific historical form, yet that even in this form it is the same yesterday and today, and has thus not only temporal but also eternal validity. Above all, we shall not be able to conceal the fact that this very question of the "here and now" of the Christian proclamation of God's humanism has the bittersweet character of being always and ever only capable of being answered, whether positively or negatively, in the form of the most comprehensive, personal, and responsible decision. So I cannot guarantee what will happen if we really do not conceal all this, but announce it openly. I can conceive that the presence and participation of Christian theologians might be found by many to be even more disturbing than, say, the presence of Communists. I can even go so far as to imagine that Communists and non-Communists might be united in considering the voice of theology in this discussion to be a serious hindrance to the profitable investigation of the question of a new humanism. Perhaps there were good reasons, forty or fifty years ago, for keeping the "preachers" at arm's length when such a discussion was taking place. I did not want to begin without calling attention expressly to the risk being run. Finally, I must make it clear that my particular contribution must be made by speaking from the position of Protestant theology.

The Christian proclamation, to come to our subject, is the proclamation of *God's humanism*. The content of the Christian proclamation could also be put in other words, for it has many facets and can be spoken in many languages. But it can also be said with these two words: the Christian proclamation deals with God's humanism. These two words alone express the idea which is decisive for the Christian understanding of man: the idea of the Incarnation. "The Word became flesh and dwelt among us" (John 1:14). According to the Christian perspective, that is the work and revelation of God—the ontological and noological premise—in the light of which man is to be seen. For the Christian proclamation is the proclamation of Jesus Christ. He is the Word which became flesh, and therefore He is also the Word about man. From the Christian perspective, man is no higher, no lower, no other than what this Word declares him to be. He is the being which is made visible in the mirror of Jesus Christ. I will try to describe him briefly, but first let me dwell on this point of departure.

1. Inherent in the Christian understanding of God's humanism, the Incarnation, or Jesus Christ is a quite specific understanding of God. This word "God" cannot be equated with the essence of Reason, Life, or Power, nor with the more popular contemporary concepts of Limit, Transcendence, or the Future. God is not—gnostically or agnostically defined—that which we think He might or might not be, nor perhaps what He ought or ought not to be. God is He whom He wills to be in His work and revelation to men. He is the almighty Lord, He who lives, in, through, and outside of Himself, in His own freedom and love. I cannot evade the glorious but hard formula: He is the triune God, who in His one divine nature is Father, Son, and Holy Spirit. This is the God of Christian proclamation, a God of loving kindness toward men. His revelation of Himself is the basis of our thinking when we speak, as Christians, of God's humanism and thus of Jesus Christ—and from Him, of men.

4

2. God's lovingkindness toward men—i.e., the fundamental relationship between God and man, which according to the Christian proclamation is to be found in God's humanism, or in Jesus Christ—is free, electing *grace*, a relationship which corresponds to our peculiar understanding of God. That is to say, the fact that in Jesus Christ God declares Himself to be the God of men is in no way grounded in the nature of God or in some necessity laid upon Him, but is rather His own sovereign, creative, merciful decision and act. Nor does it lie in the nature of man or in some capacity of his own that he among all creatures may belong to God. Nor is this something which he realizes in and with his own existence. That it has in fact happened is an inconceivable gift which he can never earn and which is in no way at his own disposal. He can only acknowledge and accept from God the fact that this is the situation. In this sovereign act of God, in this divine speaking and giving, in this free, electing grace, God and man are one in Jesus Christ, Jesus Christ is true God and true man. This is the place from which we must come to our understanding of man. Any idea of God and man, according to which their relationship to one another was by definition self-explanatory, and which might be arrived at by an analysis of the concepts "God" and "man," would be intolerable and would distort the whole picture. If we would speak as Christians of both God and man, then we must hold constantly before us the free, electing grace of God.

3. When the Christian proclamation speaks of God's humanism, and thus of Jesus Christ, since it is a question of God's free, electing grace, then it is referring to an event which has happened *once and for all time*: an event for all times and for men in every land, which took place among the Jewish people in their own land at the time of Caesar

Augustus and Tiberius. He who speaks of Jesus Christ speaks of him who stands effectively in the place of all men, or he is not speaking of him at all. The rest of us were and are not that which he is. He is, therefore, no picture or symbol of the general reality of man, with his living and dying, his suffering and triumphs. The Word became flesh. That is not a repeatable event. Rather it is an event which is eternal precisely in its datable particularity. What Jesus Christ is, what he has suffered and done, that is he and that has he suffered and done for the rest of us. As such he is Emmanuel, i.e., God with us, the living God who confronts us in His sovereign grace to make known to us the glad news that we belong to Him. This particular man Jesus Christ, therefore, is not to be considered and judged on the basis of some general preconception about human reality. Rather, every man, and the universal truth concerning man, is to be understood from this particular man.

What is man? I will now try to sum up in four points what must be said to this question from the perspective of the Christian proclamation.

1. Man is from God and for God; purely and simply an object derived from God and a subject oriented toward God; His creature, yet His creature who is free for God. Now that is the description of a movement—a history—which takes place in the allotted time given to each man in particular and to mankind as a whole. Seen in terms of God's movement toward His creatures, it is a history of the demonstrations of God's mercy. Seen in human terms, it can only be a history of man's thanksgiving, obedience, and adoration. Man finds his true existence in the event of this history. That is the word which is pronounced over him in Jesus Christ. The assertions of man's understanding of himself need not thereby be ruled

6

out as false. Ancient and modern natural science, or rather natural philosophy, teach that man is a very special and remarkable element in the cosmic-terrestrial, physiochemical, organic-biotic process of universal existence. Idealism at all times has taught that man is man because, as a knowing and moral reasonable being, he has the freedom to impress himself upon, and assert himself against, the process of nature which surrounds and opposes him. In our time, Existentialism teaches that man exists in that he, who in his natural and spiritual totality is limited, threatened, and imprisoned by an overpowering unknown, is actually able to transcend himself again and again through the very fact that he exists, and in fact is able to break through into a future which is by its nature closed to him. In the light of the Christian proclamation, that may all be true, but it is true only if it comprehends, is subordinated to, and understood in connection with, the fact that man exists from God and for God, and as God's creature is rushing toward Him and His eternal life. Everything else is only a possibility. Man's self-understanding embraces man's possibilities, not himself, not true man. Man himself, the true man, exists in that the living God exists for him and with him as his beginning and end. True man exists, therefore, in this history. That is the basis on which the Christian proclamation may make peace with classical and every other humanism, though it might also be the cause of conflict with them.

2. Man exists in a *free confrontation with his fellow man*, in the living relationship between a man and his neighbor, between I and Thou, between man and woman. An isolated man is as such no man. "I" without "Thou," man without woman, and woman without man is not human existence. Human being is being with other humans. Apart from this relationship we become inhuman. We are human by being together, by

---

seeing, hearing, speaking with, and standing by, one another as men, insofar, that is, as we do this gladly and thus do it freely. In Jesus Christ—the one who is for all the others—human existence is reflected in its vertical reality in the history of the relationship between God and man, and in its horizontal reality in a history that necessarily takes place between men. Here we stand before a question which, from the perspective of the Christian proclamation, stands over every individualistic and every collectivistic humanism, old or new. It excludes neither individualism nor collectivism. It bears on the individual and also on society, but always on the concrete individual as distinct from other individuals, and always on the society founded on free reciprocal responsibility. It defends discipline in the face of Nietzsche and freedom in the face of Marx. In contemporary terms, it defends the truth of socialism in the face of the West and the truth of personalism in the face of the East. It is an inexorable protest against any conception of man either as master or as mass. It recognizes and acknowledges human dignity, duty, and rights only in the context of the realization that true human existence means existence together with one's fellow men.

3. Still looking at him in the light of the Christian proclamation, we must go on to say that man does not exist in that reality in which he might exist, in relationship with God and his fellowmen. He does not exist in that freedom in which he was created. We speak here of a fact for which there is no explanation because it is absurd. But it is nonetheless a fact: man has strayed off his own proper way into one on which he is not able to stand or walk, but always stumbles and falls. He did not want to thank, obey, and call upon God as God, and he wanted to be a man apart from his fellow men. He despised grace. He wanted to be as God, and in wanting that he sinned,

becoming completely guilty toward God as his source and end, and toward his neighbor. In wanting that, he broke the relationship which bound him to God and his fellow man. The twofold history of his life has stalled. Thus human reality has fallen prey to nothingness and eternal death. But that is not simply man's destiny. He wanted it that way and continues to want it that way. That is why an accusation is made against man and a condemnation pronounced upon him in the death of Jesus Christ. Without question, God's humanism comprehends this accusation and this condemnation. Classical humanism, however, thought it could afford to ignore both the accusation and the condemnation. It remains to be seen whether a new humanism will ignore them. We have had many illusions about the goodness of man and his good fortune taken from us in recent times. Yet when I read Heidegger and Sartre, I ask myself whether this sort of human defiance, which despises and therefore lacks grace, is not just as unteachably sure of itself as ever. Where this defiance remains, are not these illusions sure to return sooner or later? In any case, the Church will not be able to shirk the unpopular task which the Christian proclamation has set for it of pointing out once more that the danger to human existence is greater, far, far greater than is ever willingly acknowledged. *Tu non consulerasti, quanti ponderis sit peccatum.* True man is endlessly, incurably endangered by himself.

4. The decisive word of the Christian proclamation, however, is this: This man who is estranged from his own reality, endlessly and incurably endangered, who is strictly evil and lost, this man is *sustained* by God, by the God who is true God and as such true man. Man is faithless, but god is faithful. The death of Jesus Christ is not just God's accusation against man, not just His condemnation of man. It is also—in fact it is first

9

and foremost—the victory and establishment of the complete dominion of His *grace*. God is righteous; He is not mocked. What man sows he must also reap. But God has taken it upon Himself to reap this fatal harvest. In man's own place and on man's behalf, God has sown new seed. God has placed Himself under the accusation and condemnation which stand over godless Adam and the fratricidal Cain. And God Himself, in their place and ours, became for us the true man from whose way we have strayed. God has thereby spoken. His word of forgiveness, His word of the new commandment, of the resurrection of the flesh and an eternal life. Here is the place where it becomes unmistakable that God's grace is pure, free, unmerited grace. Yet even more important, here is the foundation and revelation of the fact that God's grace endures, triumphs, rules, and is effective. The humanism of God is precisely this free, effective grace. The Church is the place where it is known and proclaimed, but this grace is for all men and for the world. It is the truth from which the Jew and the pagan live, and also the indifferent, the atheist, and he who hates his fellow man, whether they know it or not. It is the universal truth, not a "religious" truth. It is the "human condition" which is prior to all else about man. Classical humanism, in spite of its well-known relationship to so-called Christendom, never really understood this. Again it remains to be seen whether a new humanism will turn out to be new on this point. To the extent it has shown itself to date, it has revealed a remarkably doubting and unhappy face, although, or rather because it still knows all too little about man's sin, guilt, and corruption. In any case, nothing warrants being more clearly said than this: The Christian proclamation at its decisive center is gospel, a joyous proclamation of good news. It then goes on from there to say that

God's kingdom, although not yet visible, has come already, that everything has been accomplished. It goes on to protest against every form of pessimism, tragedy, and skepticism. It forbids those who hear it to walk around with a doubting, unhappy face. It is the proclamation of the hope which evil, lost man may place not in himself, but in his God, which in turn makes it possible—and this is the basis of all ethics—for him to love his neighbor.

What ought I to say, then, about the Christian proclamation as being something *here and now*? I have already given you some idea of the meaning of this expression in one limited sense by presenting the anthropological side of the Christian proclamation and indicating point by point its significance for the question of humanism. The expression "here and now," however, says not only that something is significant. It says also that this something is living, practical, and effective. Now the Christian proclamation is such that apart from its origin and subject, who is Jesus Christ Himself (and in Him it is eternally "here and now"), it is only through its own power, i.e., only through the Holy Spirit, only in faith, love, and hope that it becomes living, practical, and effective, or in short, becomes a matter of "here and now." I mentioned at the beginning the bittersweet character of this proclamation, that it meets us as a decision calling for a decision from us. So I could not by any means show you the "here-and-now" character of the Christian proclamation by reporting anything about the contemporary state and life of the Christian Church, its greater or less influence, the correct or less-correct positions which it holds. In fact I cannot show you the Christian proclamation as something "here and now" at all. I cannot hand you that on a plate. If I tried to do this, I would only succeed in leading every reader away from it as something "here and now." Were this a sermon, I would have to go on to the exhortation, "Repent and believe in the gospel." This is, however, not a sermon, but a chapter which must be brought to its end. There remains nothing more for me to do but to consider this matter from the outside and simply make the point that it would be a question of repentance and faith, and indeed of conversion, if the Christian proclamation were to become something "here and now" for the question of a new humanism. And the consideration of this subject, in order for it to be a matter of "here and now," would of course have to begin by our praying the Lord's Prayer and celebrating the Lord's Supper together, so that we might on each point and from every point of view think and speak seriously and consistently from this center, in order to be sure to arrive at the conclusion that a new humanism, if it is truly to be new, can only be the humanism of God. I need not say that it is perfectly clear to me that this would be asking too much. I simply mention it to make perfectly explicit, calmly and cheerfully, how things would look were the Christian proclamation to become all of a sudden a matter of "here and now."

2

THE SOVEREIGNTY OF GOD'S WORD AND THE DECISION OF FAITH

The subject of this chapter is not the God of this world in his variety of forms. The Holy Scripture knows about him, of course, and it would be foolishness to deny his reality and power. This god also has a word, and his word has thousands and thousands of faithful servers and heralds. In fact there are times when this word seems to drown out everything else. But our subject is not this god and it is not his word. He is not our concern. This does not mean that we have or can overcome him; but then we do not need to overcome him, for he has been overcome already. He will continue to tempt us powerfully and we will continue to suffer at his hands, but he will not devour us. We live in a freedom which he cannot harm, even if he appears to master half or all of the world, for his judgment has been pronounced and the end of his power has been determined. Therefore we need neither fear nor honor him, for he has nothing to say to or teach us. We would be fools to listen to, or take our stand upon, his word for even a moment, for then, when his time comes, as come it will, we would be destroyed along with him.

Our concern is with our God, the living God and His Word. The god of this world is only His ape, not His competitor. Our God is He who exists in and through Himself. He exists in holiness, blessedness, and glory as Father, Son, and Spirit. Yet He does not wish to be alone. In the abundance of his goodness He has condescended to call into existence the world and man in this world, and to preserve man that he might be the recipient of, and witness to, God's love. In the same abundance of His love, He wished, still more inconceivably, to be gracious to the sinner, merciful to the miserable, patient to precisely the one who is lost through his own fault. He has not diminished but enlarged His promise, even to the point of giving us the sure comfort that if we will but honor Him by placing our whole trust in Him, we shall be raised up from the dust and shall live with Him in eternal glory. Not on the basis of our own reasoning and power, but in the reasoning and power of His own Holy Spirit who leads us into all truth (in that we reflect upon our own baptism and respond to His call and teaching), we speak of this our God, the living God, and of His Word.

His Word is Jesus Christ, for God's Word is God's mediation between Himself and man which He has willed and effected Himself. Everything which takes place between God and man, from creation to consummation, takes place in the power of this mediation and thus in the power of the Word of God, working to and fro, covering heaven and earth, time and

14

eternity. This mediation and thus God's Word, however, is none other than the Mediator, "the one mediator between God and man, the man Christ Jesus" (1 Tim. 2:5). So God loved the world, mankind; therein becomes clearly visible that both our origin and our final goal are in God: that He willed to give Himself to the world in His Son and that He did so, and that in His Son He is the world's for all eternity. By doing this, He said to the world everything which He had to say to it and everything which it has to hear from Him. There is no more He can do for it than to say this and let this be heard, and it can expect no more from Him now that He has done this unexpected thing for it. For what He said to the world there, and what the world was there given to hear, is neither more nor less than Himself in all the fullness of His existence and in all the perfections of the glory of all His works. In His Son He became Himself the revealed secret of our existence. In His Son, He is, reveals Himself, and acts as He is in Himself. In His Son He demonstrates His might, establishes His righteousness, and exercises His mercy. In His Son, to sum it up, His whole action is holy, wise, and glorious, without breach or weakness, without error or contradiction. In His Son He is completely Himself and completely for and with us. The fullness of the power of the mediation between Him and us which He has willed and worked, the sufficiency of His Word lie in the fact that the power of His only begotten Son is the power of God's eternal divinity.

The sovereignty of God's Word, of which we are to speak in this chapter, is grounded and consists in this: that God's Word is His Son Jesus Christ. We are not speaking, be it noticed, simply of the sovereignty of God. We are speaking of the sovereignty of God's *Word*! This is something we should never forget: God Himself, who is for us and with us—this is the *Word* of God. The sovereignty of this our God is therefore the sovereignty of the Word of God. For a time this was forgotten and God was separated from His Word. It was thought that men should seek God and be able to find Him apart from His Word, in order to ascribe to Him the highest, most unconditional sovereignty. But the result was that then the talk concerned something totally different from the living God and His sovereignty. I have in mind the orthodox Schoolmen of the post-Reformation time and the way they followed the pagan tradition of describing God as "simple, absolute Being," going on to clothe this Being with all sorts of predicates of sovereignty.[1] The sun—namely, the sun of the Enlightenment of later centuries—showed that this sort of talk was guilty of thoughtlessness, that with this "Being" men had described perhaps the being of man, perhaps also the being of the world, perhaps even the being of the god of this world who apes the living God. But they had not described our God, they had not described Him whom we, in remembrance of our baptism and in responding to His call in the Holy Spirit, may know and praise as the true God.

There are not many left today who would doubt that in the history of Protestant theology of recent times, a deep-seated mistake has played a disastrous role, a mistake which we should do everything possible to avoid in the future.[2] Where does this mistake lie? It has often been said that it lies in the fact that the knowledge of God's sovereignty was lost in the course of time since the Reformation. But this diagnosis is

[1] Barth is referring to the seventeenth-century scholastic theology in Protestantism, which he also calls "Prostestant Orthodoxy." Ed.

[2] The reference is to the weaknesses of theological liberalism as the consequence of earlier failures in seventeenth-century theology. Ed.

correct only if it is interpreted more explicitly: It is knowledge of the sovereignty of the *Word* of God which we have long since lost and which we must try to regain. If the question is left open—Who and what is God? Where and how is He to be sought and found?—the mistake does not become visible. Then it will be little help to stress powerfully once more the sovereignty of God. Then it must, with a certain justice, be conceded to the Enlightenment and Schleiermacher, to Idealism and the various forms of theological Liberalism of recent times that they too knew quite a bit about the sovereignty of their God, who was nothing other than that "simple, absolute Being" of old Orthodoxy. The question of God's nature may not be left open and it may not be answered as it was answered by the theologians of Protestant Orthodoxy and the later heterodox theology, which was all too faithful to Orthodoxy here. Many honorable attempts to rectify that mistake have been made in vain, all because those who made them stood together with their opponents on the same ground of a false, pagan answer to the question about God's nature. On that basis, it was always possible that the sovereignty of God might just as well be understood as the sovereignty of the spirit or of nature, of a fanciful good or truth, as the sovereignty of power in itself, or finally, as simply the sovereignty of man himself. The inevitable consequence was that the Bible, which speaks of the sovereignty of a wholly different God, had to be watered down or twisted in its most important assertions. Then there arose the threat of a crippling and corrupting danger, as an esoteric secret, as a theory which in intention was made "in faith," of a picture of a God who was indeed sovereign, but sovereign only in the way in which that "simple, absolute Being" can be sovereign—that is, a God who was not able to bring in a new creation, not able to do wonders, hear prayers, forgive sins, rescue from death and make blessed, not sovereign as is the living God proclaimed in the Holy Scriptures. From this there arose a stench of godlessness, never fully dispersed in spite of all well-intentioned and partially effective reactions, which ran through the history of Protestant theology. Let us not deceive ourselves into thinking that we have now got rid of it in our own time. We will only be rid of it when we learn again to seek God in His Word, and to seek His sovereignty in the sovereignty of His Word, which is to say, in the sovereignty of His Son Jesus Christ. If I understand it correctly, that is the decisive thing which the Reformers of the sixteenth century learned and which they have to teach us as something new today. Again, if I understand it correctly, a repristinization of the theology of the Reformers would be of little help to us; rather, in order to be true to them, we will have to go further than they themselves went along the road which they have pointed out. Even more than the Reformers did, we must let *God* and His *Word* be *one*, with more emphasis, more joy, more consistency, and we must let Jesus Christ be even more self-evidently the one Mediator between God and man.

The actual sovereign act of the Word of God is its existence as the man Jesus Christ, in which God's eternal Son united our nature with Himself, made its creatureliness His own, and also took upon Himself the curse which was due it, in order that He might share with it in turn His divine glory. In that He thus becomes ours, we cease to belong to ourselves and become His. In that He thus becomes weak, He becomes in fact strong. In that He thus gives Himself up, He becomes our Lord. In that He was thus made sin, He acts as the only holy one. Right in His condescension and abasement He rises up above every creature and every God. He lets himself be taken

18

prisoner in the power of the god of this world, and in doing so strikes him down and dispatches him once and for all. That this is so is confirmed and revealed by His resurrection from the dead. But that which was accomplished in God's Son Jesus Christ in our nature was done in our place and therefore for us. That was once for all our reconciliation too, our justification before God, our sanctification for Him, our becoming heirs of eternal life. On Golgotha, *everything* was accomplished. With this sovereign act is everything (really everything!) which stands against us beaten down. By it is dissolved every obligation we owe to the god of this world (really every one!). Every (really every!) anxiety which we could have in this world was removed in Him. He, Jesus Christ, stands as Victor over our sins of yesterday, today, and tomorrow, over the hosts of temptation, over the horror of death and hell. And with this sovereign act there is erected the kingdom in which we may already, here and now, be children of the Father because of His eternal Son. For in taking our place, he is no longer apart from us. He is become the Head of the body of which we are members. He is become our Advocate at the right hand of the Father, the first-born of many brothers. And the completion of the sovereign act of God's Word, the work of the Holy Spirit, is that it may stand as true and valid, that we may want to and actually do live on the basis of all this: He not without us! He with us, and in this way and thereby, God with us!

Everything else we might think of when we speak of the sovereign act of the Word of God can be only a repetition of this first thing, only the confirmation of this one thing, only the reflection of this original. The sovereignty of the Word of God is always the sovereignty of Jesus Christ. When the Church recognizes in the witness of the prophets and the apostles its own foundation, the source of all wisdom and the norm of its teaching and life; when it dares in obedience, in the exposition and application of this witness, to proclaim God's Word itself; when it baptizes in the name of the Father, Son, and Holy Spirit; when it calls men to the Lord's Supper as to the visible proclamation of the death of Jesus Christ and thus to the true spiritual food of His body and blood given for us; and further, when this witness runs and works in the Church itself and in the world; when it awakens to life but also executes justice; when it brings peace but also causes discomfort, struggle, and suffering; when it gives answers but also raises new questions; when men are called out of the world so that they are sent forth again into the same world as sheep among wolves; when the question of the just state is raised by the free gospel in an unavoidable way—then all of that, together and in each of its parts, insofar as it happens in truth and not in mere appearance, all of that is the one sovereign act of the Word of God as it unfolds, reaches out near and far, works directly or indirectly. Always it is He Himself, Jesus the Lord, who is acting in all that. And in all that, in turn, the criterion of truth can and must lie in the question, whether He Himself, Jesus the Lord, is the One who is at work and can be understood and honored as such.

Just what is the *sovereignty* in this single yet manifold act of the divine Word? I hope I will not completely miss the mark by trying to understand and to characterize it under three headings.

1. The sovereignty of God's Word lies in its omnipotence. Let us hasten to add: in the omnipotence of the love in which God is God and in which He has turned Himself toward the world in His incarnate Word. It is precisely this power or potency, truly qualitatively distinguished from all other good

or evil potencies, which is omni-potence: power over every-thing, the power of the Creator, Preserver, and Ruler of all things. Because God Himself is the Word, this and no less a power stands at the disposal of His Word. This and no less a power is the power of Jesus Christ. But as His power this is also the power of Holy Scripture, the power of preaching and the sacraments, the power of the confession of His Church, the power which is secretly or openly effective wherever He Himself, the Son, is at work through the Spirit. The Word of God is not one power among others. It does not have to fear any limitation because of them. There is no sovereignty of nature or history opposed to Him. Nature and history and their kingdoms do not stand on the same plane with Him. Rather, they stand at His command. Therefore the Word of God can be trusted. Therefore the Word of God is truly com-forting and certain, infallible and reliable. Therefore its prom-ises, commands, judgments, and blessings are not empty talk, but creative deeds. Therefore is it the seed of the new man. Therefore it creates and upholds the Church. Therefore the Holy Scripture and preaching grounded in Scripture, there-fore the sacrament is living and powerful. Therefore the world, simply from the fact that God's Word is in it and spoken to it—quite apart from the question of whether or not the world accepts the Word—is now a different world, a world inwardly overcome, a world already laid at God's feet. Therefore we have nothing to fear in this world and every-thing to hope for. "In the world you have anxiety, but be of good cheer: I have overcome the world" (John 16:33). *Illicitum non sperandum!* We are not allowed not to hope!

2. The sovereignty of God's Word is distinguished by its exclusiveness. There is one Mediator between God and man. The light of this One, who is that, unmasks the others who

want to be but are not that. The Word of God is indeed for all. It does include all areas of existence. But only this One is the Word of God. And therefore, the Word of God travels a solitary road. It stands in the witness of Holy Scripture lonely among religions, world-views, myths, and ideologies. Therefore Christians must also, again and again, be lonely. God's Word does not harmonize with other words, for there exists no second and third, but only one Word of God. Thus it cannot be heard together with other words, nor can it be heard inclusively. It can be heard only exclusively, or else not at all. Other words can be only its echo or a response to it, giving a contradictory or acknowledging answer. As God is unique, so is His Word. This can be used as a test: only in this exclusiveness is it that omnipotent Word, "the Word of power, by which God upholds all things" (Heb. 1:3). The unique comfort is the "comfort in living and in dying."[1] Only as brothers of the one Son of God will we become new men. Only to Him, to the One, is that power given which no longer allows us to sink in anxiety and care. Put the one Word side by side with others and it is become already powerless, comfortless, and without creative might. But it would not be the Word of God that we were hearing at all if it were put side by side with others. The sovereignty of the Word of God is distinguished by the fact that it has no competitors.

3. Finally, the Word of God is sovereign in that it is spoken and reaches us in divine freedom; not the blind freedom of fate, ruling by some unknown law over gods and men, but in the freedom of the divine mercy and patience. This is the freedom which gives freedom to others, which gives us and allows us our freedom, which asks of us that we place

---

[1] From the first question of the Heidelberg Catechism of 1563. Ed.

22

ourselves at its disposal in freedom—not forced, not pushed, not overpowered, but in adoration. But that is to assert the priority and superiority of the divine freedom over this freedom of ours! The Word of God is true before we come to know it to be true. Its choice rests upon us and it is its work which happens to us also in the moment in which we choose a lie in misuse of our freedom. We have then become liars about God's Word, recognized and exposed as liars and rejected by Him. Even as condemned and lost men, against our will, we cannot help but give the honor to Him, His righteousness, and also His mercy which we have pushed away from us. We are then by grace itself exposed as being graceless. But it happens in the fullest sense, by the power of His righteous and merciful judgment, when in adoration we choose the truth. We may and ought to choose, but it is His decision, the decision of the Word of God, just when and where our choice is the choice of truth in adoration. Then our choice has in the fullest sense the character, the significance which is ascribed and assigned to it by God's merciful decision. It is the grace of God's Word itself that makes it possible for us to recognize it as true and to receive it as grace. The same Jesus Christ is free to be our Judge and our Savior. And so also in the witness of the prophets and the apostles, also in its proclamation by the Church, the one Word of God is free to bind and to loose, to blind and to enlighten, to damn and to save. Once more, it would not be the Word of God which we were hearing if we did not feel constrained to recognize without qualification its full sovereignty in this sense as well.

We could not speak of the sovereignty of the Word of God, however, without immediately speaking also of ourselves, namely of the decision of faith. It lies in the very nature of that sovereign act (as surely as this act was the act in which the true God became true man), that it is related to, and directed toward, us, that we are the objects of this act and to that extent participate in its completion. We participate in the way in which the creature, in the way in which man can participate in God's nature and work: as recipients of a gift, as sharing in the power of His wisdom, sharing in the fruit of His work, yet in this subordinate role sharing nonetheless in His sovereignty and its exercise. We would have to retract everything we have said, we would have to deny God, if we were to leave ourselves out of the picture here, if we were to forget or to keep silent about the fact that in and under the sovereignty of God's Word we ourselves are also included, that we ourselves are supported, preserved, and moved by it, and thus and to that extent are also raised up and glorified by it. Is it not truly God's Word that is the mediation between God and man which God has willed and effected, and has not God in His Word made no less than His own self to be the Mediator between Himself and us? Then how could that Word "return to him empty" (Isa. 55:11)? Has not His Son for all eternity made our nature His own? Does He not live and reign at the right hand of the Father in our flesh? Then He is not without us. He has us with Him. Thus He lives our life in the glory of God. That is our share in the sovereignty of God's Word. It is raised up, it is hidden in Him who is the Word of God. But just in this way it is truly our share in that sovereignty.

Who are we who have this inheritance? Men? Yes, without doubt, men! But "what is man that you think upon him and the son of man that you care for him" (Ps. 8:5)? What is man under the sovereignty of the Word of God? No abstractions now, please! No absolute claims for any self-made, independent, human understanding of the self! No anthropology isolated from Christology! What is man, who has such a share

24

in this, that Jesus Christ wished man to share in Himself? What is man, man without which Jesus Christ would not be Jesus Christ, man who therefore would not exist were it not for Jesus Christ? Here there is only one answer: This man is man in the *decision of faith*. Everything else which man is in addition to this, that he is a creature, a reasoning, sinning, mortal creature, that he has a conscience and an idea of the true and the good, that he receives from his fellow man the concrete task of his life, that he is subordinate to, and responsible for, the order of the state, that as man he lives in self-contradiction and yet is not without religious possibilities and opportunities, not without God in this or that conception of the word—all that is well and good, but all that is only secondary, only a predicate to the real subject. Man is what he is and he is everything that he is in the decision of faith. For in the decision of faith he moves toward being ascribed and given that human nature which Jesus Christ has united to Himself, that He might establish in it peace between God and man. In the decision of faith, he stands before God as the man God intends and in the way in which God wills to have him. In the decision of faith, he exists and stands before us in his true nature. No matter how it may be with all other determinants of man, in the decision of faith and only there is he his true self as the true man!

The decision of faith is the human correspondent to the Word of God. The Bible has no knowledge of man in general. It knows only the people Israel and the Church, only man as one called or being called into this gathering. But that means: it knows man only in the decision of faith, and everything else it may say about him, good or bad, comes always and ever from this. And if the Bible has not borne testimony to us of the sovereignty of God's Word in vain, then we too have no other way in which to know man than this, and only as a supplement to this we can wish to know everything else that is to be said about man.

Faith: the truth of our existence founded on, and discovered in, Jesus Christ—what does it mean? Let it be said in the simplest words, with the words of the Heidelberg Catechism: "that with body and soul, both in living and dying, I am not my own but the possession of my faithful Savior Jesus Christ." Put in other words: that I depend on God's Word; that my focus, my center of gravity, my support lies not in me but in Him; that I let myself be nourished, enlightened, and ruled by Him; that I grant Him his right over me, over my pride and also over my humility, over my confidence and also over my insecurity, over my stupidity and also over my wisdom; that the Word be loud while I remain quiet; that the Word lead and I follow; that the Word be great and above, while I be small and beneath; that the Word of God stand in its sovereignty and thus in its omnipotence, exclusiveness, and freedom, whereas I in all those secondary determinations, I in the completely natural and historical concretion of my humanity, I for the first time and only in this relationship to the sovereign Word of God find my *true* manhood! This is faith: that I let Jesus Christ be for me what I am not and cannot be for myself: my truth, my goodness, my righteousness, my salvation; that I let the Word of God be my God, my Creator and Preserver, my Lord and Savior. And this, therefore, is our share in the sovereign act of the Word of God; this, therefore, is our true manhood.

But it is a question of the *decision* of faith. It could also be said: It is a question of the life, the reality, the event of faith. The word "decision," however, says in the clearest way what must be said here: Faith always means choice, crisis,

26

transition. We believe as those who have been torn away from the abyss of unbelief and yet who stand on its rim. Therefore, "I believe, O Lord, help my unbelief!" (Mk. 9:24). We believe and apprehend in faith the possibility of our true existence by being preserved from our own impossibility, from being rejected and lost. We trust instead of denying. We entrust ourselves to One instead of to many. We surrender instead of asserting ourselves. "Not my own, but the possession of my faithful Savior Jesus Christ!" It is in this reversal, in this turning toward and in the turning away from all else which is its concomitant, that we believe. Persistence in neutrality could only signify the choice of our own impossibility, since faith is our only true possibility. And that is valid whether one thinks of faith in the moment of the act of believing, or in the continuity of the life of the Church or individual Christians. Faith is always decision. It is always in the decision of faith that we have a share in the sovereignty of the Word of God and are therefore truly what we are.

Who decides here? Without hesitation we must confess that, first of all and fundamentally, it is not we ourselves who decide. In every case, if we believe, we believe in the consummation of the sovereign act of the Word of God. In every case, it is the work of the Holy Spirit which happens to us. We have noted above that the Word of God is sovereign by the fact that this happens in divine freedom. We have no power over it; it is not at our disposal. We have no claim upon it and we have done nothing to earn it. For in that it happens, in the adoring choice of the truth, in that we believe—all such claims (as that we have the power to be able to believe) and also all such demands (as that we must accomplish our own believing) are struck to the ground. In faith we stand before God as sinners, saved by the fact that our sins have been forgiven us. In faith we acknowledge that we deserve wrath and rejection, the wrath and rejection which Jesus Christ has taken upon Himself in our place, in order to place us, whose life is glorified in Him, in the light of the divine grace. We can only choose as men who have already been chosen! Where is left any room for boasting, as if we had wanted and accomplished something ourselves? And where is room left for any sort of law, according to which we might have to construct in whatever way our own salvation and our own service to God? But by the very fact that, when we believe, God Himself in the sovereignty of His Word has decided about us, faith as our own act can have no other character on earth than that of a decision! The decision of faith takes place on the earth and thus in fear of the divine judgment and in need of forgiveness for past and future sins. It means always that we must dare to give and be responsible for giving the command of God's Word a quite specific exposition and application, and this exposition and application can be dared and undertaken in responsibility, only in great humility and only in great joyousness. But it must be responsibly dared. We must obey, and we can obey only in the form of such a decision, and therefore only in such an exposition and application of the Commandment, carried through in fear, humility, and joy. We will thereby be left with the impression that the accomplishment of the decision of faith far surpasses our insights and strength. And we will thereby often enough seem to others to have presumed too much for ourselves. But we are not questioned about the wealth of our own strength. Rather, we are questioned about our obedience and only thus about what we have made of the pound entrusted to us. It is not so bad to appear presumptuous as it is to persist in neutrality under the guise of humility, which in fact means already the decision of unbelief. How could the decision of faith be made without self-criticism and without being open to the critique of others? But under all circumstances, it must take place, and it may—no, it must—then take place with assurance, in the face of all self-criticism and the criticism of the whole world, looking forward with head held high to the Judge who is also our Savior. How else could we fallible and erring men be obedient?

> But He who loves us without end
> Restores what we have squandered,
> Brings joy where we create distress,
> And leads when we have wandered;
> Alone because it's His desire,
> His own paternal goodness pure,
> He takes us sinners to Him
> As His beloved children.

It would be taking an all too high or an all too low view, in any case a fundamentally perverted view, of the sovereignty of God's Word if for the sake of the Word we wished to evade the decision which it demands of us, out of a false fear of it or from a false trust in it. It is the Word itself which commands us to make a decision.

In the decision of faith, we must—no, we may dare to lay hold of the possibility which is given to us to be the children of God. That we do so dare is the event which happens under the sovereignty of God's Word. Everything else which may be asked of us is measured by this, that its final and ultimate significance lies in this risk. Where there is no question of this risk, where the question, to what extent this risk is demanded of us, is quite foreign, there the decision of faith still stands ahead of or already behind us. That is when we should be concerned with the question whether we are still (or once again) grasped by the decision of unbelief. We are asked about this risk in our private lives. We are asked about it by our neighbor, in whom Jesus Christ comes to us as the merciful Samaritan to the man fallen among murderers. We are asked about it in our jobs, be they what they may. We are asked about our confession of faith in the Church, and the Church itself is asked about its confession, which means concretely that the men therein assembled are asked if they will acknowledge and affirm by word and deed the possibility given to them of being children of God and thereby members in the body of Jesus Christ, which is a gift not of our own making. We are asked about this decision also in the political realm—as surely as this realm also belongs to Him to whom has been given all power in heaven and on earth—whether and to what extent our thinking, speaking, and actions, our unavoidable political responsibility have taken place in faith, as the decision of faith, as humble and resolute apprehension of God's promise; we are asked whether they are, in fear and trembling, the choice of that which is essential to the life of the children of God. With these words we have already pointed out something which cannot be stressed too much in our day!

With respect to its compass, no fundamental limits can be put on the decision of faith. Its compass must always be precisely as large as demanded by the sovereignty of the Word of God under which it comes to pass. Why may it not be first of all always a decision of our hearts and consciences, our knowledge and our wills, an act of theological reflection? But woe to us if we wish to determine arbitrarily that it is and ought to be sufficient for it to remain an intention and a reflection, in the realm of the spiritual—let us say, for example, in the realm of persisting in what is perhaps a very radical, very dialectical, very eschatological theology.[1] Or we might select other realms, such as the realm of the personally private, the personally moral, or indeed the personal religious confession! Or even the "realm of the Church," where it is well known that the most extraordinary things are mightily spoken, heard, and felt concerning God, the world, and man! Woe when matters come to such a pass that arbitrary limits are placed on the decision of faith, which seek to limit it to the sphere of knowledge and conscience, the sphere of that which is private and personal and to the sphere of the Church! A limited decision is as such not the decision of faith. Every "inner" in this matter points to an "outer," indeed to a new and as such ambiguous, dangerous, compromising "outer." Every honest, theological dialectic as such makes clear as its end and goal a most undialectical Yes or No, in word and deed! He who believes is no reasonable fellow. He who believes does not run away. He who believes is not afraid that his decision might become visible. He who is concerned about his alibi in the face of temptation and danger, which are surely to be expected from "out there," does not believe at all. Such a man might be quite convinced that the highest possible triumph of faith took place when he was nicely "inside" somewhere, saying nothing and doing nothing. But in fact it is "outside" where the Devil goes about like a roaring lion, and we have been summoned to resist him, in soberness and watchfulness, not to run away from him. That would be a pretty sovereignty of the Word of God which would allow us or even demand of us that we replace the decision of faith with a voluntary and harmless pious dialectic without goal or purpose! But no

[1] Barth is here referring to "Barthians." Ed.

more proof is needed here: this non-obligatory and harmless dialectic has nothing to do with the sovereignty of God's Word. No matter how Christian it may look, that sort of dialectic belongs to the kingdom of the god of this world. Because it is effective, it is perhaps the greatest triumph of the god of this world. I warn my readers: It is precisely of this god that I am not speaking!

The decision of faith is the necessary proclamation of, and witness to, the sovereignty of God's Word. When the witness of the Christian Church is powerless, this is always related to the fact that that has not been recognized. Even the proclamation of the sovereignty of God's Word must be powerless when it is not made alive by the decision of faith, when it persists in that neutrality which is secretly already the decision of unbelief. But that which is not proclaimed in the decision of faith can by no means be the sovereignty of the Word of God. And let us not forget: the decision of faith, precisely as proclamation of the sovereignty of God's Word, is at the same time the proclamation of true manhood, of true humanity, we may say. Indeed, this is alone that which is honestly human and pleasing to God and which shares in the promise of eternal life. We stand today in horror before the phenomenon of a Europe, a so-called Christian Europe, which is threatened with the loss of its humanity. The problem lies not with those forces which would take its humanity away and would lead it into chaos. The problem lies in the fact that Europe itself has chosen not to decide, that it does not dare to choose and thereby has chosen evil, which means it has chosen inhumanity. But honest choice and decision, and thus a decision for humanity, exist only as the decision of faith, and the decision of faith, in turn, exists only under the sovereignty of God's Word. How has it come about that

---

Europe has not been better instructed by the Christian Church concerning the sovereignty of God's Word, and thereby seems to know so little about the decision of faith and a resolute decision for humanity? Is it that the Christian Church itself knows too little of the sovereignty of God's Word? And therefore itself too little of the decision of faith? It is more essential today than ever, for the sake of our eternal as well as our temporal salvation, for the sake of the Church of Jesus Christ as well as the just State, to ask, seek and knock: *Veni creator spiritus!*

3

THE PROCLAMATION OF GOD'S FREE GRACE

The words "free grace" by their very juxtaposition indicate first and last nothing other than the nature of Him whom Holy Scripture calls "God." He is the Subject of the "mighty acts" to which Holy Scripture gives direct, authentic, and full witness, and in the celebration and proclamation of which the Christian Church has the ground of its existence. The expression which is used in the sixth thesis of the Barmen Declaration,[1] "the proclamation of God's free grace," therefore,

[1] The Barmen Declaration of 1934 was the manifesto or confession of faith of what came to be called the Confessing Church in Germany—those Christians who stood together on the basis of this confession in resisting Hitler's attempt to control both the government and the preaching of the Church in Germany. Barth was a leading figure in this movement and the Confession, written at a meeting in Barmen, is clearly marked by his theology. Barth, a

does not mean anything else than that which Rom. 1:1 calls, in the briefest of formulae, "the gospel of God." God Himself, the one true God, who spoke to the prophets and the apostles, is free grace. And therefore because free grace is a joyous thing, the proclamation for which God commissioned the prophets and the apostles, the proclamation of the Christian Church, is gospel, joyous news.

This God is the God who in Jesus Christ created heaven and earth, and man on the border between heaven and earth, the God, who, again in Jesus Christ, has accepted man—man who had fallen away from Him and been lost, but not lost to Him—and also the whole world which He had created. This is the God whose will, plan, and purpose it is, once more in Jesus Christ, "to bring together all things" (Eph. 1:10) at the last day, in which everything, and man in the midst, will be revealed in the glory of Him who at the goal of all His judgments and ways will be all in all. This God is God in such a way that He is free grace in all His deeds. In unfathomable freedom He chose Abraham and no one else, Isaac and not Ishmael, Jacob and not Esau, David and not Saul, just so that

Swiss citizen, was expelled from Germany several years later and accepted a chair of theology in Basel.

Thesis six of the Barmen Declaration reads:

"'Behold I am with you always until the end of the world' (Matt. 28:20). 'God's word is not bound' (2 Tim. 2:9).

"The task of the Church, on which its freedom is based, is to deliver, by means of preaching and sacrament, in the place of Christ and thus in the service of His own word and work, the proclamation of God's free grace to all people.

"We reject the false teaching, according to which the Church, in human self-assurance, may put the Lord's word and work to the service of any arbitrarily chosen wishes, goals and plans." Ed.

He might be in unfathomable grace the God of the whole people of Israel, and finally, in the promised seed of Abraham, not only the God of the Jews, but also the God of the Gentiles, our God. So He is; so He has revealed Himself to be. The name Jesus Christ is the name of this divine nature of His.

God is God by virtue of the fact that in His eternal Son, and therefore from all eternity, He was, is, and will be the God of men, who loved, loves, and will love men. He did this, does this, and will do this in freedom, for He is sovereign, He is majesty. He is the omnipotent God. He has aseity, as the old theologians used to say: He is sufficient unto Himself and He needs no other. His loving is in no way a form of needing. But all this is grace: He looks down—even more, He steps down from the unsearchable height of His godliness into the depths of an existence eternally different from Him, into the depths of the being of heaven and earth, into the depths of human existence, in order to create it out of the void, and to sustain it over the abyss of nothingness "out of pure fatherly goodness and mercy." Even more, He did this in order to make it like Himself, in order to be one with it, in order Himself to be man in His Son, and so the effective Reconciler of man, the powerful Savior, the mighty Helper against guilt, in which He wraps Himself, and from death, to which He has surrendered Himself. And further, He did this in order to make Himself the guarantor of the future of man and His universe, to make His own eternal life the promise and hope of this creature of His.

This is God's free grace: not some mere "property" of God's, beside which He might well have others as well, not some activity of God's, which could occasionally be overlooked because apparently He was also active elsewhere in some left-handed way. No, God's free grace is God Himself in

His most inner and essential nature, God Himself as He is. That is God's secret, as it is now already revealed in Jesus Christ to those who hear and accept Him as God's Word, and as it will someday be revealed to all when the veil will be removed from all eyes, when it will be revealed in its fullness, clarity, and blessedness to the eyes of all His creatures, even those who are now blinking, squinting and blind, even to our own evil and perverted Christian eyes. If it was right to let the Barmen Declaration begin with the sentence, "Jesus Christ, as He is witnessed to in the Holy Scriptures, is the one Word of God which we must hear and which we must trust and obey in life and death," then it was also right to close it with the statement that the task of the Church is to deliver the proclamation of the free grace of God. If Jesus Christ, attested to in the Holy Scriptures, is the unique Word of God, then there is no getting around the fact that our word, the word the Church has been commissioned to speak, can be no other than precisely this message, "the gospel of God" in this sense.

God's free grace. Because it is free grace, the proclamation of the Church cannot begin with some sort of human need, concern, care, lack, or problem, nor may it take from these its content or direction. Rather, in the face of all these, it may and must announce God's glory, His justice, wisdom, and kingdom. So surely as Jesus Christ is Lord to the glory of God the Father (Phil. 2:11), so surely must we His friends walk in His footsteps in this matter. Surely the first three petitions of the Lord's Prayer and the first four Commandments also point to this: the God who is God in the highest. But while this side of the matter should be considered and granted full validity, the other side ought also to be seen clearly: it is free grace. *Soli Deo gloria* refers to no high idol, no divine egoist, no eternal "crab apple," but to the Father of mercies and God of all comfort

(2 Cor. 1:3). It refers to Him who has made it a point of honor to create and preserve us men, to reconcile us to Himself, to redeem and perfect us. It refers to Him who has made our business His own, who is zealous about His divine justice in order that there may be genuine human justice under His heaven upon our earth. It refers to Him who really does not sweep our human needs, concerns, cares, lacks, and problems under the rug, but who takes them up, makes them His own, and answers and solves them better than we can know or desire. It refers to Him for whom no tear is too small: "He takes it up and puts it aside," Why should He want to have men who are free for Him and thus free from themselves? So that they may be really free. And all this is so, just as surely as the last three petitions of the Lord's Prayer and the last six Commandments have their whole goal in the fact that grace is really grace, the word and work of the one true God addressed to us and our human existence.

God's free grace. Because it is free grace, the proclamation of the Church cannot deal with any characteristics, capacities, points of contact, and the like which might be credited on the human side, or with any human potentialities or merits which should be taken into consideration. It is grace for creatures to whom God owes nothing, nothing at all. It is grace for sinners, who have deserved God's anger and nothing else. We never have it: it can only be shared with us ever anew. We experience it in no other way than in bowing before it and allowing it every time to begin with us as though we were nothing and as though nothing had happened before this. It comes to us as a gift, and that without presupposition, reservation, or condition. And when we have it—when we have grace as we go our way, be it in a Christian congregation, or in our proclamation and theology, or in a single man's lonely

38

acts of obedience and trust—then we have it only to plead, to pray, and to give thanks for it. And we must plead, pray, and give thanks as though it were ever totally new and quite foreign to us. Only thus, only in this freedom, is it also commanding, sanctifying, costly grace. But don't forget for a moment that it is grace precisely in this freedom, given to us just as we are, as powerless creatures, sinners lost through our own fault, who walk in the shadow of death—really given to us.

Grace means Emmanuel, God with us, in such a way that we men—for in the incarnation of God's Word, in the cross and resurrection of Jesus Christ, it is we about whom it was universally decided in the middle of human history—we men are not given over and left to ourselves, to our misery, even to our own inclinations. Grace, which asks not a word about what we are, what we have, what we bring along with us; grace, which leaves us no other hope than in that which is undeserved, God's free grace accepts us men, just as God's Word has accepted flesh, our flesh. It has accepted us already in Jesus Christ, long before we in turn could think of accepting it. It comforted us already in living and in dying, before we became aware of it, and quite apart from when or how we might have become aware of it. God's grace concerns us men, and being a man means being one of those who have been met by God's grace. Jesus Christ would not be the Word through whom all things were created if we could withdraw from this objective, ontological circumstance, which is the prior reference of all our decisions.

God's free grace. Because it is free, it has and keeps its throne and locus in Jesus Christ Himself alone, and therefore the proclamation of the Church may and must be the proclamation of Christ, and nothing else. He is the just one, the holy

---

one, the eternally living one. He is the prophet and the word, the priest and the sacrifice, the king and the kingdom. He and no other, He and nothing along with Him. It is always a denial of His work and an execrable idolatry to seek to repeat His sacrifice in some sacrifice which is offered by human hands, to venerate and worship Him, the true God and true man, in another form than His own, to place a Mary as mediatrix of all grace, and thereafter a whole chorus of such mediators of grace, alongside Him, to associate a human vicar with Him, the Lord of His Church, to ascribe such a possession of grace to a man that on the strength of it he could obtain further grace for himself and others.

Man is not and never will be a co-redeemer, a second center, a secondary source of grace. In fact, the man who through grace believes in grace, with his loving and hoping, with his obedient doing and suffering, will reject such an idea with horror. Grace would then obviously not be free grace. But after this has been said, we must add: It is free grace in that Jesus Christ, in whom God's grace alone resides, has not, does not, and will not remain alone. He has called His apostles, the prophets having already perceived His promise beforehand. He has called many through their Word; He does it still, and He will do it again. Why? So that they may all put their hope in Him alone; so that they may bear witness to all creatures that He alone is their hope; so that "grace for the sake of grace" may be recognized as the great law of all Creation by these few, and through these few by the many, and through the many by all. He called His apostles, therefore, so that there might be: His community, gathered together and protected by Him; baptism into His death; the Lord's Supper as participation in His life; faith in Him, and with it, of course, participation in His anointing; service in His service as prophet, priest, and king; unassuming proclamation of His lordship over the whole world; and His promise to all men, indeed, to all creatures of heaven and earth. Grace, in its whole freedom, is grace in that it is this comprehensive gift: the gift of the one Jesus Christ, first to His witnesses, then through them to His Church, then through the Church really and truly "to all people."

God's free grace. Because it is free, it has the power to do its work even among us miserable sinners, to set its word even in our foolish and wicked hearts, and even on our filthy lips. David the adulterer and murderer was no hindrance to it, nor was Peter the denier, nor Saul the persecutor. Even the Church, which one might sometimes have reason to think of as the darkest of all dark places, even the Church is no hindrance to God's grace. We may trust it as being more powerful than us Christians, than the ocean of nonsense which precisely we Christians commit individually and collectively. Why should we not rely upon it? It is and will prove itself once again to be much more powerful than everything which the children of this world, in their absurdity and disobedience, can set against it. Yet let us not forget that the Lord called them wiser than the children of light. Who knows what sort of "last" ones might turn out to be first again? The proclamation of the Church must make allowance for this freedom of grace. *Apokatastasis Panton?*[1] No, for a grace which automatically would ultimately have to embrace each and every one would certainly not be free grace. It surely would not be God's grace.

But would it be God's free grace if we could absolutely deny that it could do that? Has Christ been sacrificed only for

[1] "The restoration of all things," expressing the belief that every man will finally be saved. Ed.

our sins? Has He not, according to 1 John 2:2, been sacrificed for the whole world? Strange Christianity, whose most pressing anxiety seems to be that God's grace might prove to be all too free on this side, that hell, instead of being populated with so many people, might some day prove to be empty! But if the freedom of grace is preserved on both these sides, something else has to be said: that whoever and wherever he may be, man is not only reached and blessed by grace, but in one way or another he is taken by grace into its service. Grace calls us into the decision of faith. Grace allows us no idleness, no neutrality, no standing aside. Grace allows no excuse because of our impotence, unworthiness, or sins, not to speak of alleged disappointing experiences with other men, supposed personal experiences, or bitterness about our ecclesiastical or worldly surroundings, however justified they may be. Grace has thought of all that long ago: our own insufficiency and failure, the whole dubiousness of the manner and actions of our fellow men, even "the partly disturbing, partly pitiable condition of our dear evangelical Church," as an old Basel liturgy put it, even the stupidity and wickedness of the world with its indifference and insipidness, with its atheism and idealism, with its transgression of all ten Commandments, with its profiteers and greediness, with its old and new Nazis and whatever else there might be.

Grace does not ask for our judgment of ourselves or of others. Grace simply wants to have us: to have us as we are in the Church and as they are in the world, so that we might be its witnesses. More is not demanded of us; for the whole law is included in this one thing. This one thing, however, is asked of us. Grace proves itself to be able to overwhelm us in that it demands that we honor and praise it and thereby announce it to others in all circumstances, even the worst possible inner

42

and outer situation. We must call their attention to this: they are God's just as surely as we may know that we are God's. Even in the midst of hell, grace would still be grace, and even in the midst of hell it would have to be honored and praised and therefore announced to the other inhabitants of hell. It is not free for nothing, but it is also not grace for nothing. We should certainly not know it if we were of the opinion that we could stop short of announcing it.

God's free grace. Because it is free, it is not bound to human ways and means. The proclamation of the Church has to make that apparent with complete clarity. The area of "the Church's concern" is not a prison, but a platform open on all sides for the word of God's grace. The language of the Church, theological language, the edifying language of Canaan, may not be the fetters of this word, nor may the history and tradition of the Church, with their special "events and power, forms and truths," with their dogmas and confessions, with their liturgies and polities. The fact that men in the evangelical Church once quarreled over *est* and *significat* in the Lord's Supper, over the omnipresence or the heavenly absence of the true body and blood of Christ, and really never settled it, does not necessarily mean, for example, that we have to take up these positions again today, warm up that fight again, and battle it through to the end. We ought to reckon rather with the fact that God's grace could have long since led the Church forward and put questions and tasks before the Church that are quite different from those of the sixteenth century. We must reckon with the fact that it can always be at work outside the walls of the Church and can be announced even by quite other tongues than those which have been given to us. Its being so free brings fresh air again and again into the Church. We need this fresh air, and we should not try to shut it out with the holy games of our churchly speaking and behavior, and above all not with antiquarianism—otherwise we shall be calling up the old demons again! The Lord God could be more liberal than we think or like. But we are speaking about God's liberalism and therefore about the freedom of grace. Because it is grace, it allows and opens up many human ways and means—only those which belong to grace, of course, and therefore never without strict commanding and forbidding, but many ways: old and new, usual and unusual. Because it is grace, the old ways, "the affairs of the Church," the language of Canaan, the tradition of the Church have their right and a certain necessity, in their place, and they ought to be heard and respected in all circumstances. Because it is grace, there may, under the radiant humor of God, even be "confessionally determined churches," which may tell God, for a few more years or decades, what it—namely, what the free grace which was finally recognized corporately in 1934[1]—might signify for its future. Grace is patient. But grace is also stormy. Because it is grace, it will point out and open up new ways to the Church, which dare not cut itself off from walking in these new paths: new ways of seeing and addressing men concretely; new ways of soberly estimating human things in general and also political and social things, fearlessly calling them by name in their contexts; new ways in which it will—and this is a hundred times more "worthwhile"—pray with them in German and not in translated Latin; new ways of singing a new song unto the Lord, as it has seriously enough been commanded. Jesus Christ yesterday. Indeed, God's grace has preserved us in all those things which were necessary

[1] Reference is to the situation of the Confessing Church and the Barmen Declaration. Ed.

yesterday and should become living matters again; but Jesus Christ today too, right now! May God's grace neither refuse us the orders nor deny us the right to do those things which are obviously necessary in the present-day situation of Europe and the world.

God's free grace. I want to mention one last thing. Because it is free, it reaches beyond the present form of man and his world, and so the proclamation of the Church must always be the proclamation of a new heaven and a new earth in which justice dwells, the proclamation of the mystery of the future of Jesus Christ. God is not hidden to us; He is revealed. But what and how we shall be in Christ, and what and how the world will be in Christ at the end of God's road, at the breaking in of redemption and completion, that is not revealed to us; that is hidden. Let us be honest: we do not know what we are saying when we speak of Jesus Christ's coming again in judgment, and of the resurrection of the dead, of eternal life and eternal death. That with all these there will be bound up a piercing revelation—a seeing, compared to which all our present vision will have been blindness—is too often testified in Scripture for us to feel we ought to prepare ourselves for it. For we do not know what will be revealed when the last covering is removed from our eyes, from all eyes: how we shall behold one another and what we shall be to one another—men of today and men of past centuries and millennia, ancestors and descendants, husbands and wives, wise and foolish, oppressors and oppressed, traitors and betrayed, murderers and murdered, West and East, Germans and others, Christians, Jews, and heathen, orthodox and heretics, Catholics and Protestants, Lutherans and Reformed; upon what divisions and unions, what confrontations and cross-connections the seals of all books will be opened; how much

45

will seem small and unimportant to us then, how much will only then appear great and important; for what surprises of all kinds we must prepare ourselves.

We also do not know what Nature, as the cosmos in which we have lived and still live here and now, will be for us then; what the constellations, the sea, the broad valleys and heights, which we see and know now, will say and mean then. What do we know? We think we know sometimes, when we see the high peaks at dawn or when we hear certain chords and melodies. But we do not know even then. We ought not to act as if we knew this or that, even in an elementary way, when we are only guessing. That God's grace is free grace will be impossible for us to overlook at this point, even if we might overlook it elsewhere. But this much is sure: it is also here, and precisely here it is grace. We know just one thing: that Jesus Christ is the same also in eternity, and that His grace is whole and complete, enduring through time into eternity, into the new world of God which will exist and be recognized in a totally different way, that it is unconditional and hence is certainly tied to no purgatories, tutoring sessions, or reformatories in the hereafter. Whatever may come, when everything passes away one day and becomes new, God's grace will come, and with it God's realm and the Judge too, "who has presented Himself for me before God's tribunal and has taken from me every curse." He will come who has already come, recognized and confessed by His own. And today too, He is revealed for all—"Behold, I am with you always, even to the end of the world"—and revealed as He who was, is, and shall be for everyone. Thus He was, is, and shall be: the Fulfiller of God's Word spoken in Him; the Redeemer of the world which He has reconciled; the Revealer of the good will, the plan, and the council of Him who created heaven and earth

---

and all that is therein; the Answer to the great and small questions of our life and our common human history, the really troubling ones and also the superficial ones, simply the questions at hand; the Righteousness of God's power over us and all creatures, now secret, but later on to be revealed. We are not merely of this opinion; we know it, as certainly as we know Him who is the same yesterday and today, Grace would obviously not be grace if, with respect to the end of all things and their new beginning—the end and beginning of all things signified to us by our death—we were not allowed to know this. But we may know this, and we may face what comes "with head held high." He is our hope.

The heart of this whole matter is that the task of the Church, according to the Barmen Declaration, is to deliver this message—the message of God's free grace. And along with this goes the fact that the freedom of the Church is grounded in just this task.

For this message to be delivered, one must be conscious of oneself as acting under a commission. Even viewed externally, it is something too high, too bold, too rare and precious to allow us the opinion that we might start talking about it in the way one may make any statement about human existence, on the basis of observation, experience, reflection, as duly acquired convictions made on one's own responsibility. Its content warns us in a decisive manner of the falseness of this opinion, for this message is precisely not a statement about human existence—it becomes that only subsequently. It speaks, rather, about God: the God of Abraham, Isaac, and Jacob, the God and Father of Jesus Christ, the God who spoke to the apostles and the prophets. It speaks of the nature and actions of this God; it speaks, therefore, about that which has not been imagined, thought out, and experienced, but can only be heard, learned, and repeated in the school of this God's own Word, as did the prophets and the apostles.

The sixth Barmen thesis says of the proclamation of the message of the free grace of God that it occurs "in the place of Christ and therefore in His own word and work." This message is related to and in fact comes from Him of whom it speaks. Jesus Christ is not only its subject, but its inner source, not only its material cause, but also the cause of our knowledge and confession of it. That means, however, that it must be understood again and again as that which has been and must be received from Him, wherever it is proclaimed. Those who proclaim it may not force it into some system or philosophy, some world-view or outlook on life. They cannot come to terms with anyone who presumes to have Jesus Christ at his disposal, or who would try to classify Him within his own conceptions, no matter how good, deep, or pious. One cannot deal with the free grace of God the way one can deal with a principle. The heralds of free grace cannot advertise themselves as, or behave like, purveyors of a principle. In fact they must deny the "human self-assurance" which seeks to "put the Lord's word and work to the service of any arbitrarily chosen wishes, goals and plans." The message of free grace has never remained pure, has always been perverted into its opposite when it has been put into some sort of service or framework which is foreign to it, whether worldly or spiritual, philosophical or theological, and when it has thus been proclaimed with a certain human self-assurance. It can be announced only "in Christ's place" (2 Cor. 5:20, "on behalf of Christ"), that is, only in the service of His own word and work, only in the acceptance, repetition, and confirmation of the testimony by His prophets and apostles to Him. "The word of God is not bound." It is not bound

48

to some previous understanding of our existence, situation, or position in the history of the Church, of thought, or of the world. It is itself that which must be understood prior to understanding all of these. Otherwise it is not the Word of God. Otherwise it is not the Word of His free grace. It is a reflection of its content that it finds its own human heralds and clothes them with its responsibility, its truth, its wisdom, and its authority, that the Church is charged with its proclamation and has absolutely nothing at all of its own to proclaim.

In this way is the Church charged with this proclamation. And so it has no boast of its own. This message is as new and foreign and superior to the Church as it is to all the people to whom the Church is supposed to proclaim it. The Church can only deliver it the way a postman delivers his mail; the Church is not asked what it thinks it is thereby starting, or what it makes of the message. The less it makes of it and the less it leaves on it its own fingerprints, the more it simply hands it on as it has received it—and so much the better. The Church is also not asked whether its own power, faith, skill, and knowledge are adequate for the transmitting of this message. It is required simply to use all that as it is and as best it can, but it must put all this completely and without reservations in the service of this message. And the Church is not questioned about the visible or invisible, great or small success of its deeds. It is supposed to toss its seed about—only let it see to it that it is this seed—like the sower in the Gospel, in the holy thoughtlessness for which Goethe once found fault with this sower. Its way is shown to it. It only needs to go along it. He who founded and sent it out, and continues to found and send it out, bears its responsibility. Let it but go along that path. Let it but live in that commission. Surely the Church need not then worry about the coming day.

The Church exists by living for this commission. Thus, it does not exist as an end in itself. It has no line of retreat into a churchly subjectivity. It flees neither into preaching nor into the sacrament, neither into exegesis nor into dogmatics. It strikes forward when it preaches, and it strikes forward when it baptizes and celebrates the Lord's Supper. Its exegesis is assault and its dogmatics is also assault, or else they are not worth the time and trouble they take, nor the expensive paper on which they are written and printed. The Church does not escape into prayer either, but it prays in order to work. And for just that reason it will also not escape from prayer into all kinds of relief work or politics. The reason why it does not escape is that in no respect is it there for itself. It exists alone for the message of God's free grace. It goes with it into the whole world; with it, and for its sake, to make it concrete and clear, then certainly also in the form of relief work and (let us hope, clever and bold) political decisions. It delivers the message as God's message "to all people." Therefore the Church itself is there for all people.

Again, the Church is not asked whether or not the people accept it, or whether or not it deserves their confidence. It is not asked to account for their piety or their godlessness, for their orthodoxy or their idolatry, and therefore not even for the stand the people take with respect to the Church. It is not asked whether it might lose itself in being there for the people. It has no diplomacy or strategy to carry on with respect to them. "When Jesus saw the people, he was moved with pity for them; for they were tormented and exhausted like sheep without a shepherd" (Matt. 9:36). That is the only thing that counts and is interesting and urgent. The people are "just people," as they have always and everywhere been. They are tormented and exhausted because, in their piety and godlessness, in their orthodoxy and idolatry, they have no shepherd and they go astray. The shepherd they lack is Jesus Himself, and therefore the message of God's free grace. When Jesus saw these people, He was moved with pity for them. There, in His discipleship, is where the Church belongs. It is simply there for these people. Otherwise it cannot be there for God. It cannot be the Church at all, except by repeating the great turning of God, to which Christians as well owe their existence, toward the trespassers and the lost, and thereby making the free grace of God visible. In this sense, the Church can be the Church only as the people's Church; and only as the Church for the people and in the midst of the people can it be a confessing Church.

The Church exists by living for this commission. And the message must have this addressee: all people, the people, as they were, are, and will be. For what the people need, what God, who loves the people, has intended for them, is just this message in its whole fullness, depth, and boldness; the Church has no other task in addition to proclaiming this message. Those to whom this message is addressed are simply the people, the quite ordinary people, with their serious and their childish concerns and needs, with their confused consciences, their dullness and illusions. Anything else besides just going to these people is certainly not the commission of the Church. If the Church does not love the message of free grace (if it stands apart from people with too many scruples, if it meets them with too many reproaches), if it is afraid of that message and is too pious and moralistic for people— what is the Church then? Nothing, nothing at all!

And now we shall touch upon the last thing which the sixth Barmen thesis dared to say at that time in fine defiance of the threatening attacks and successful infringements of the totalitarian state: the Church's own freedom is founded upon its commission, and therefore upon the message of God's free grace. But remembering the situation then should not lead us to think that the freedom of the Church lies in standing touchily in a little corner, playing games and sulking, able and required to converse with neither the state, nor society, nor the arts and sciences of the surrounding world. The Lord can surely let the world say something to the Church from time to time, which the Church must allow the world to say of it. The freedom of the Church is its right and duty to exist in these surroundings, in joyful and modest openness to the outside. This freedom is based on something the world does not have, which the world can neither give it nor take from it: its commission, and therefore, the message of God's free grace, and therefore its Lord Jesus Christ, and therefore God's manifest and living Word. This freedom still remains with the Church, even when it lives out its assignment quite imperfectly. The commission as such remains; the Church is able to change nothing, objectively speaking, in the message of free grace, in spite of its faults and weaknesses; but it must then put up with the fact that this message is also—and in fact, first of all—its own judgment. Jesus Christ remains; God remains; and because of Him, the freedom of the Church remains at all times, the freedom to be reformed of all the deformations of which it may have been or still is guilty. God's free grace which it is privileged to announce to all people is its own most personal hope.

This message, which the Church, even the lazy and disobedient Church, is commissioned to proclaim, is of such a nature that it (even in its weakest and most distorted forms) will always have something original to say to the people that they would certainly not hear otherwise, either in lectures or in school courses, at the movies or at party meetings, in their conversations or in talking to themselves. The uniqueness, the plain extraordinary character of this message is inexhaustible, and that is what will make the Church free and will establish the right and the duty of its existence again and again. The message of the free grace of God is also of such a nature that it does not let the Church which has fallen asleep sleep too long. It is an incomparable trumpet, which continues to have at least a potentially awakening effect, even in the hands of an incompetent trumpeter. It can break out of its concealment at any time and make the Church free again, procuring for it anew its rightful place in the sun. Above all, it is of such a nature that even when proclaimed in a stupid manner it has a way of producing, suddenly and anew, now here, now there, men who are in fact free, that is, nimble, humble, questioning, seeking, asking, knocking men, and in this sense free Christians, Christians who dare to begin in a truly fresh way at some place or other, as "the law of the spirit of life" (Rom. 8:2) commands them to, despite all worldly and churchly meshes and clamps. They do this as though it were something which had never yet happened in the doctrine, life, and order of the Church and its relationship to the world, plowing ahead with something new—despite clergymen, Pharisees, scribes, despite tyrants, despite the temper of the times in politics, society, and science, despite Mr. Everything!

As long as this kind of free Christian arises, the Church will be freed again and again, and it will prove time after time its right to exist. And this kind of free Christian will arise again and again, as surely as the message of free grace is the commission of the Church, which it cannot throw off, and which no one can take from it. The message of God's free grace includes all that within itself. But the Church shall not rely on what comes with it: its originality, its latent power to awake the Church to life and action, and not even the rising up of those free Christians. As it is a question of its own freedom, it must rely on the message itself. From this message comes the right, the duty, and the freedom of the Church to exist as the Church in the world, as the *ecclesia semper reformanda*, without pretensions, but also without fear before all Christian and unchristian demons. We must ask about this message; we must orient ourselves about it; it is the gift which people of the Church and their servants, the *ministri verbi divini*, must awaken anew in themselves wherever the freedom of the Church is at stake, wherever it is pressed by cares. It is the gift whereby they may remain the Church—or rather, may now more than ever become the Church. Everything else besides, all ritual, confessional, or constitutional questions, and whatever else may be are secondary and can rightly be answered only from this point, or not at all. God protect us from all hobbyhorses and pigheadedness! One thing only is necessary. It appears that we understood this in 1934 when we closed the Barmen Declaration, in harmony with the first thesis, with the sixth thesis about the free grace of God. It remains to be seen whether we understand it still or even better today than at that time, grasping it anew because it is something which can only be grasped anew.

4

THE AUTHORITY AND SIGNIFICANCE OF THE BIBLE: TWELVE THESES

1. A proposition concerning "The authority and significance of the Bible" would have substance as an analytical proposition only if it were to express in other words a situation which is beyond all uncertainty and therefore had as its presupposition just this situation.

Ask a child why, among many women, he calls this particular one his mother, and all he will be able to say will be only a repetition and affirmation of the very thesis for which he has been asked the reason: "But this *is* my mother." That she is his mother is for this child the situation beyond all uncertainty. In the same way, every substantial proposition (i.e., one not merely apparent, but truly appropriate to the subject) concerning the authority and significance of the Bible expresses a

---

55

situation about which no discussion is possible, a circumstance which, being grounded in itself, speaks for itself and therefore can only be elucidated by means of repetition and affirmation. This circumstance is the simple fact that in the congregation of Jesus Christ, the Bible has a specific authority and significance. He who would speak substantially in this matter must be aware of this intrinsic, fundamental relationship between Bible and congregation. Whether he himself stands within or without the congregation, whether he personally acknowledges or denies this specific authority and significance of the Bible, if he does not want to speak so as to completely miss his subject, he must be prepared to see and take account of this purely given relationship between Bible and congregation, and that in this business, on the decisive point, there can only be analytical propositions which express this relationship without trying to establish its foundation.

For Christian preaching and confession of faith, for the proclamation of the congregation to the world, everything depends on the fact that the heralds of this message be conscious that in this matter of the authority and significance of the Bible, to which they must appeal with every word they say as Christians, they can only make an accounting with analytical propositions, since the circumstance of this relationship, well established in itself, stands clearly before them. The apologetics of the congregation can only consist of having no fear before these analytical propositions. On the contrary, the congregation must openly confess them and thus become actively engaged in that faith and obedience which it asks of, and expects from, the world. I have begun with these remarks bearing on the question of form rather than content in order to make it quite explicit from the very beginning that in the exposition of the question of the authority and significance of the Bible which I have undertaken, neither from the inside nor from the outside will I be able to open up the circle of truth in which we should move. On this matter, at the decisive point, I can make only analytical statements. If I am to speak honestly about this matter, I do not know any other way to go about it.

2. The presence and Lordship of Jesus Christ both in His congregation and in the world has its visible form, in the time between His resurrection and His return, in the witness of His chosen and appointed prophets and apostles.

The time of the congregation, our time, is the time between the resurrection of Jesus Christ and His return, between the breaking-in of the new age and the passing away of the old, between the "It is accomplished!" of the reconciliation of the world with God which took place in Jesus Christ and the "Behold, I make all things new!" of the definitive revelation of this event. There is a presence and Lordship of Jesus Christ also in this our intermediate time, and it has not just one, but many forms. "All dominion in heaven and on earth has been given to me." The kingdom of Christ has no boundaries. All mission to the world, all international politics of the Church, is only the subsequent proclamation of this victory already won, of this King already enthroned. There is but one place where all this is known and acknowledged. That is the congregation founded on the biblical witness, the witness of the prophets of the Old Testament and the apostles of the New Testament. This biblical witness is the visible form of the otherwise hidden presence and Lordship of Jesus Christ. "You shall be my witnesses." "He who hears you hears me." And then, "Behold, I am with you always even to the end of the world." All these refer to the particular bearers of the witness upon which the congregation is founded. "So we are ambassadors on behalf of Christ; for God is making his appeal through us." Paul was referring here to his election and calling. But as Jesus Christ belongs to Israel, so the prophets of the Old Testament belong to the apostles of the New. In this old and new witness to Christ, the presence and Lordship of Jesus Christ in his congregation is visible, not hidden. The Holy Spirit is the presence and Lordship of Jesus Christ Himself in the visible form of this witness. This witness is the Word which the congregation heeds "as the light which shines in the darkness until the day breaks and the morning star arises in your hearts." The congregation, the Church, can exist only in a movement from and toward this Word. If the Church were to come from anything else or move toward anything else, it would simply cease to be the Church. By walking in the light of this Word, Christians are "children of light." Through this Word they are comforted and encouraged. Through this Word they are bound together, looking back in one faith, looking ahead in one hope, on the road leading from yesterday into tomorrow in one love. This is the Word, the prophetic-apostolic witness as the visible form of the presence and Lordship of Jesus Christ Himself, which makes the congregation to be the first fruits (*aparche*) of the whole of humanity and a sign erected between heaven and earth of mankind having already been gathered and summed up together (*anakephalaiosis*) in Jesus Christ as its head, which is yet to be made visible.

3. The truth, power, and validity of the witness of these men is that of their subject: they bear witness to Jesus Christ, and thus to the work of the gracious God, as the beginning, middle, and end of all things.

What distinguishes the witness of the prophets and the apostles, so that it can have this significance for the existence of the congregation and its proclamation to the world? After all, they were men as fallible as we are, children of their time as we are of ours, and their spiritual horizon was as limited as ours—in significant ways, even more limited than ours. Whoever enjoys that sort of thing can again and again demonstrate that their natural science, conception of the world, and also to a great extent their morality cannot be binding for us. They told all sorts of sagas and legends and at least made free use of all kinds of mythological material. In many things they said—and in some important propositions—they contradicted each other. With few exceptions they were not remarkable theologians. They have only their election and calling to commend them. But this counts! Their many-sided testimony has, in its own way and in its own place, one and the same center, subject, and content: Jesus of Nazareth, indicated and anticipated in God's covenant with His people Israel, born at the end of the divine judgment on Israel's unfaithfulness, together with the new people, His disciples and brothers, the Christ of the Jews who as such is also the Savior of the Gentiles. The Old Testament witness (to Yahweh and His Israel) and the New Testament witness (to the one Jesus Christ and His people) agree: in this confrontation of the gracious God with sinful man, the history, the action which constitutes the center of all created things, which contains the secret of their origin in God's creation and their goal in a new creation, has now taken place. This confrontation is the counsel and will of God for His creature, the meaning of all existence in time. The Bible asserts this by the fact that it speaks of Jesus Christ. That God and man, in the power of God's free grace toward sinners, belong together as do Yahweh and Israel, as do Jesus and His people, this is the word of comfort and exhortation which the biblical witnesses address to other men. Having this center, subject, and content, their witness has a special truth, power, and validity over and above other human words which may be perhaps more significant in other ways. The congregation is the place where the peculiarity of this witness and the election and calling of these men are understood and respected.

4. Insofar as this subject and the relationship of these men to this subject are unique, their witness in this time is the single normative form of God's Word for the congregation and for the world.

The prophetic-apostolic witness, through which the congregation of Jesus Christ is established, is the single normative form of the Word of God for that congregation. There are many things in the heavens and on earth, but there is only one God. There are many ideas about God, but there is only one true knowledge of this one God, true because derived from God's self-testimony. There are many events, powers, forms, and truths which are important, worthwhile, and indispensable for us men, but there is only *one* Word of God, only *one* Jesus Christ, in whom the confrontation of the gracious God with sinful men took place once for all. And because not all, but only these particular men are the elected, called prophetic and apostolic witnesses to Jesus Christ, there are many hidden forms but only this *one* visible form of the one Word of the one God. Only in this form is God's Word finally, decisively normative, binding, and authoritative. The Church of Jesus Christ acknowledges the unique Word of the unique God in this uniquely visible and uniquely normative form. In this knowledge, it sets the biblical canon.

The establishment of the canon is its confession of God's election and calling of His witness. Since its knowledge in this matter as in everything else is a limited, human knowledge, preliminary and perhaps in need of expansion and correction, its confession in this matter as in everything else can have no final character nor be intended as more than a provisional conclusion. The specific limits of the canon have in fact, in ancient and modern times, been a matter open in principle to the possibility of better instruction in the future concerning the concrete extent of that canon which the Church knows as the unique, normative form of the Word of God. But by no means does it follow that the Church can therefore take account in practice of any other normative forms of God's Word. Human reason and its historical productions, the movements and decisions of general world and spiritual history, the spirit and tendencies of various times, even the history of the Church itself (its written and unwritten traditions and orders, the voices of its ancient and more modern Fathers, its general and specific convictions raised up as dogma in the past and those certainties and exertions which rule today)—all this has indeed its own truth, power, and validity. But all this cannot have the truth, power, and validity of the normative Word of God for the Church. All this cannot be taken up by the Church *pari pietatis ac reverentia* with the biblical witness. The congregation is under no compulsion, nor is it guilty of an arbitrary choice, when it chooses to be ruled finally and decisively by the sole means of the witness of the prophets and the apostles and thus by Jesus Christ. Indeed, in this it exercises the freedom given to it in its knowledge of God. And it is its task and mission to tell the world that for the world as well there is no other visible and, in the strict sense of the word, authoritative Word of God, no other binding form of the divine dominion, than the Holy Scriptures.

5. The witness of these men proves itself to be God's Word by the fact that it summons, conforts, and exhorts the Church

in the name of the risen and returning Jesus Christ, and there-with gives to its proclamation to the world actual freedom, direction, and fullness, the character of a Word which is first and last.

The knowledge that the prophets and the apostles are the witnesses—the only witnesses! of the visible and therefore normative Word of God can of course be proved, but it can be proved only by the fact that the prophets and the apostles do indeed with their human words speak God's Word, by the fact that God's Word is indeed heard through the words of its human witness. The old theology quite rightly called this actual self-proof of the authority of the Bible "the witness of the Holy Spirit." But it is open to misunderstanding if it is further called an "interior" witness, as though it were not also exterior. By speaking in this way, the Church failed to dis-tinguish clearly enough this self-ratification of the authority of the Bible from a magical incantation. The heart of the matter, quite soberly, is that the biblical witness in the name of the risen and returning Jesus Christ to God's grace toward sinful men issues in fact as a summons to men and in fact finds a human hearing and produces a human response of obedience. Men are comforted by its proclamation of peace and are exhorted by its commandment. Again, to be quite sober about it, the fact of the matter is that these men find themselves made heralds of this Word, and that their own words, awakened by this Word, do receive freedom, depth, fullness and life, and a particular biblical orientation to God's glory and kingdom and to man's thankfulness. They find themselves, in fact, set in a position to confront the world as the deliberate bearers of a Word of primary and ultimate validity.

The witness of the Holy Spirit is the event in which all this

THE AUTHORITY AND SIGNIFICANCE OF THE BIBLE

happens. But all this takes place in the Christian congregation. The Christian congregation takes place, comes into being, and consists in this event. And this is the witness of the Holy Spirit, the self-attestation of the biblical authority: that all this does in fact happen, that the Church is and may thus live. Properly speaking, only the congregation can give a competent answer to the question whether the Bible is really and truly the Word of God, and its answer can only be that the Church itself respects and obeys the Bible and invites the world, as its own act, to share in this same respect and obedience. It can only convey the proof of the Spirit and of power. It is always the consequence of its own unfaithfulness—namely, the consequence of the fact that it is not yet or is no longer the Church under the Word of the Bible—if this its proof does not enlighten and convince as it could and ought. The cognitive question in this matter, then, is decided by matters of fact and only by matters of fact. Where the Spirit of the Lord is, there is freedom, and where freedom is, there is the city set on a hill which as such can never be hid, the light which lights all who are in the house.

6. The biblical witness as God's Word expounds itself. It corresponds to its human character, however, that in expounding itself, it lays claim on the service of human exposition.

Where it happens that the biblical authority authenticates itself by actually obtaining a hearing and obedience, there it has evidently spoken understandably and been understood; there, evidently, exposition of the Bible has taken place. In this case, there has arisen a picture of that concerning which the biblical witnesses speak, and it becomes possible, with the help of their words, to think through after them what those witnesses thought. In this way, an independent repetition of the picture painted with, and the thoughts indicated by, their words is reached. The Word of God in those human words is then contemporary for them who hear those human words; it has become transparent for them, in spite and in the very lack of the contemporaneity of those human words. How else could it come to pass that the words of this witness have summoned, comforted, and exhorted other men of other times and made them heralds of God's Word as they heard it proclaimed in this witness? This having happened, we must say that the words of the biblical witness of these other men manifestly became clear. He who says "witness of the Holy Spirit" says "exposition of the Bible."

Who is it that expounds the Bible? We answer with the ancient axiom which must be the axiom of all hermaneutics: *Scriptura scripturae interprets*. With respect to the Holy Scriptures, that means: These writings, as God's Word in human words, expound themselves, are in themselves—i.e., in the coherence of the so differentiated and complex reality given them by their common subject—everywhere perfectly clear and transparent. But this clarity (*perspicuitas*) of the Bible, grounded in its authority, is no inherent property, but rather a moment, a particular determination of that event in which the biblical witness speaks up and wins a hearing, thereby giving the Christian congregation its origin and its support. The Bible does not expound itself in such a way that the men to whom it expounds itself can be idle listeners. It expounds itself in such a way that these men—in accordance with their collective and individual capacities, and finally and decisively "according to the measure of their faith"—are drawn into the service of this exposition. The Word of God spoken to them in the human words of the prophets and the apostles is certainly not at their disposal. Rather, the transparency of these human words is God's free gift. But this gift is placed in their hands, and it is theirs to make their own insofar as they will make use of it. Thus the exposition of the prophetic-apostolic witness becomes a human task and activity. So also the exertion concerning the biblical texts and the reproduction of the picture seen and the thoughts used in these texts, so also the exertion to render these contemporary through independent repetition—all become a service which must be performed if the Church is not to honor the authority of the biblical witness with lip-service only, if the Church is to be the Church at all. Where the Church is truly the Church, it is bound in this service of human exposition, corresponding to the human character of the biblical witness.

7. Sound exposition of the biblical witness takes place when the fixing, pondering upon, and assimilation of its human (literary-historical) form is determined by a thankful remembrance of God's Word heard already and a joyful expectation of hearing that Word anew.

The task of biblical exposition is first of all the same as that of all exegesis: it must establish, reflect upon, and assimilate a literary-historical form as such. That is to say, it must work out the wording of the texts and the meaning of those words. It must bring to light the perspective and conceptual world of the author of a given text, in its narrower and broader context, and, as exposition of this text, it must take care to translate his meaning and intention. That is, it must try to reproduce this meaning and intention in the corresponding perspectives and conceptions of the exegete's own time. Exposition means commentary. It is self-evident that an honest commentary upon the Bible can have no other aim than to let the biblical texts speak for themselves anew. And it is just as self-evident that it must assist the text as a whole, and therefore also word for word, to its right to do this. In this sense of the word, all sound exegesis is "biblicist."

The biblical texts do not wish to be understood as a historical-literary "source" for any sort of knowledge. Rather, they lie before us as the witnesses to the Word of God which establishes and rules the Church. The sound exposition of these texts, therefore, must take place in the context of harkening to that Word of God which they want to make known to the Church, whether that Church be in its beginning or already established, and which they want to make known to the world through that Church. Sound exposition of these texts demands, therefore, that the expositor be in a position to place himself at least hypothetically in the shoes of the Church which hears these texts. It is this place which gives one the quite specific position from which alone the biblical texts are to be understood and expounded. It will probably not be possible in practice for him who only hypothetically stands in this place to truly occupy this position and thus have the capacity for true understanding and exposition. However that may be, the position which comes only from standing in this place is definitely not one which provides a person with a previously obtained knowledge about a Word of God "available" in the human words of the text. That was the naturalistic error of the doctrine of Inspiration of the late seventeenth century and of those who laid the groundwork for this doctrine in the ancient Church. God's Word is never "available" for anyone. God's Word is God's Spirit, who blows where He will. God's Word happens when God is spoken of, *ubi et quando visum est Deo*. That God has already spoken His Word in the sphere of the canonical witness, and that He has thereby promised to speak anew in the same sphere, this is something known by that congregation which lives under this witness.

The position of the expositor, demanded by the congregation's standing where it does, is therefore *remembrance*, and indeed a *thankful* remembrance of the Word of God already heard, and it is *expectation*, indeed *joyful* expectation of hearing God's Word anew. The sole rule for "theological" or "pneumatic" exegesis is that the expositor, who otherwise does what every sort of expositor does or ought to do, harkens to God's Word in this sense. The peculiarity of theological exposition consists alone in the fact that the expositor moves within the area commanded by these texts when he is dealing with the biblical witnesses.

8. The "authoritative" (in the above sense) existence of the biblical witness is the curative guarantee that in the life of the Church and in its proclamation to the world there can ever anew be a true confrontation between the gracious God and sinful man.

Where the authority of the biblical witness is acknowledged, a lively confrontation and conversation will follow ever anew within the life of the Church itself and in the relationship between the Church and the world. The Bible will have something to say to the Church and, by its agency, to the world, questions to put and answers to give. "On behalf of Christ" it will be able to teach, direct, and rule the Church and, by its agency, the world. But this means: in the Church itself and in its relation to the world, a real meeting can take place between the gracious God and sinful man, a repetition of the Old Testament situation—Yahweh and Israel—and a repetition of that of the New Testament—Jesus and His people. In this repetition, however, the "communion of the Holy Spirit" will fall away wherever the special and considered authority of the biblical witness disappears, wherever men put it on the same level with Church tradition, and

67

consequently place it under the control of the ecclesiastical teaching office. It matters not whether the latter is borne by an ordered or other hierarchy, the mighty words of leading theologians or the mass of believers. The way of the Roman Church culminating in the *Vaticanum* and the way of modernist Protestantism culminating in the proclamation of the sovereignty of the universal religious self-consciousness are twin paths, in this important matter as in other areas.

The modernist Protestant can easily be a Catholic tomorrow, and vice versa. There is no fundamental difference whether Christ vanishes behind the figure of the infallible successor of Peter, on the one hand, or behind the universal character of every man as a child of God, on the other. Either way He has ceased to be Lord. In either case we have a flock without a shepherd, a Church with none standing over and above it, no Teacher, no Judge, no King, which has nothing to hear and will listen to nothing. That would be a Church that knows everything better than everyone else and has none who could correct it, a Church given over to itself and its own conceit. And that would also mean a world to which this Church had nothing to say, which had certainly no proclamation to receive from it and which would be quite right in declining to acknowledge the claims of such a Church. Where the special and considered authority of the biblical witness is not acknowledged, a meeting between the gracious God and sinful man can only take place in a shattering of the dominion which is there in force. Precisely in order that this might not have to come to pass in the life of the Church and in its relationship with the world, Jesus Christ commissioned his apostles and thereby confirmed also the prophets: "You shall be my witnesses." Communion between God and man means a confrontation between them, that characteristic

68

confrontation in which God is gracious to man and man stands as a sinner before God. This confrontation is guaranteed by the subordination of the Church to the Scriptures and the dominion of Scripture over the Church. That is why this subordination and dominion may not cease to be real and effective for even a moment.

9. The practical significance of the authority of the biblical witness lies in the fact that the Church is willing to account in the final analysis for its whole life, its order and services, its confession and teaching, its preaching and instruction and its posture in the life of peoples and governments before this witness, and to give place to it as the source and norm of all maintenance and renewal.

Where authority is, there is obedience. The authority of the biblical witness is the authority of Jesus Christ, the Lord of the Church and the cosmos, He who is the subject of this witness. The Bible, therefore, is no "paper pope" and its authority is not of the legal kind. It is, rather, a spiritual authority. It is Jesus Christ Himself, whom the Bible calls and to whom the Bible witnesses as Lord, and it is the Spirit of the Bible, who exercises and commands authority inside the Church and by the agency of the Church in the world. That the biblical witness has authority includes the fact that the Church is ready and willing to set its own life in the service of this witness. There is in the Church no form of constitution, order or office, worship or community life, confession or dogma, theology or instruction, which might lead us to the conclusion that, prior to the witness of the Bible, the Church must measure itself or let itself be put in question by some such form because of its antiquity or especially hallowed tradition, the memory of some person or this or that experience connected with it, or because of local or national peculiarity or familiarity, or some dominant spirit of the times, or because of its political or social utility. The Church can have many and good reasons for taking a stand in these matters, but it may never seek to make itself secure from being questioned from the biblical witness, just why it took this particular stand and whether it might not better take some other stand.

This rule comprehends as well—and indeed here they have truly their place—the Church's decisions and postures toward the outside: its proclamation to the world, its relation to general human society, to its culture, to the life of the people and to the government. Let the Church reflect with care on the fact that in all these things it is responsible to no one ultimately except to its Lord Jesus Christ as He is witnessed to in Holy Scripture. To Him it is fully and strictly responsible. Let the Church guard the freedom which He gives it! And what is more important, let it grant Him His freedom to teach, direct, and rule the Church as He wills! Let it not interfere with Him through any despotic conservatism or through any despotic revolution! Let Him be given room in both directions! Neither the Church itself nor the world about it determines that which must fall and be replaced by something new, or what must be held on to and preserved in the Church's own life and in its relation to the world. He determines this, and He does it through the voice of the prophetic-apostolic witness to be heard anew every century and even every morning. Again, the Church might have many other good and weighty reasons on both sides in any of these matters. The decisive reason, however, the final source and highest norm of all preservation and renewal is He alone who said once for all time: "He who hears you hears me!" The practical significance of the biblical authority lies in the Church's listening and never ceasing to listen to them to whom Jesus said this.

10. The Church, together with its commission with respect to the world, stands or falls with the presence and Lordship of Jesus Christ in the form of the authority of the Bible as defined.

The last three theses are designed to call attention to the fact that the matter of which we have been speaking does not have a neutral character. It cannot just as well be denied as affirmed, for it is a matter of all or nothing, the question of whether to be or not to be. By the presence and Lordship of Jesus Christ, in the form of the authority, as now defined, of the biblical witness, the Church stands, lives, and exists in the appropriate humility and glory in which alone it may. After what has been said, there can be no question but that when the presence and Lordship of Jesus Christ in the form of the authority of the biblical witness falls away, the Church can, in turn, only fall. To say it pointedly: When the Church lacks the authority of the biblical witness, it and its proclamation to the world can only dissolve into pious smoke and all sorts of religious and moralistic odors. What would be left would be but a psychological-sociological phenomenon which would be boring, meaningless, and uninteresting to God, to the world, and especially to all those who would seriously be Christians, which would have no deeper right to exist. No one can prevent another from taking his stand elsewhere than in the Christian Church and thus from thinking and speaking from out of some other context. But whoever believes himself to be standing within and not outside of the Church takes on co-responsibility that the Church stand and not fall, and co-responsibility that the biblical authority as here defined stand as the foundation of the Church, being neither forgotten nor denied.

11. Christian theology, together with its service to the

Church and also its right to its particular existence among other disciplines, stands or falls with its being willing in theory to honor the authority of the Bible as defined and in practice to make it fruitful.

Theology is also involved in this question of standing or falling. It may fall independently by excusing itself from the theological task and turning into a study of religion. In that capacity, it might also begin with the authority of the Bible and do what it could. But theology is not free to be Christian theology and to serve the Church as such and to lay claim in this capacity to its right to exist among other disciplines, and at the same time to have no theoretical or practical use for the authority of the Scriptures in the sense we have given. Theology is theology (and not pseudo-theology!) to the extent that it renders an account to itself, the Church, and the world concerning the authority of the Bible in the direction pointed out, and to the extent that it knows how to make this understanding fruitful in practice in all its branches. If it is not prepared to do this, then its service in the Church has long since become derangement and its existence within the university long since a shadow-existence. That the public is perhaps not yet aware of this does not alter the fact of the matter. No one has to be a theologian, but he who would be one should be a proper one. And to be a proper theologian depends on his being willing not to avoid the scandal and foolishness of "the principle of Scripture" or, better put, not to avoid the grace and distinction which theology also experiences from the authority of Scripture. Rather, he will confirm concretely that the fear of the Lord is the beginning of wisdom by accepting this grace and distinction thankfully and without fear.

12. The ecumenical unity of the Christian Church and its

theologians is a truth or an illusion insofar as the authority of the Bible as defined is respected or not respected.

This final proposition touches directly the problem of the "authority and significance of the social and political message of the Bible for today." What is the ecumenical unity in which we must stand together in order to discuss this question with one another in a meaningful way? Ecumenical unity must obviously lie in our being in accord about this fundamental question of the authority and significance of the Bible in and of itself. On what other basis could we be in accord in even asking the question about the authority and significance of the social and political message of the Bible for today? After what I have said about the Church and theology, I cannot very well go on and conclude with the enlightening assertion that the ecumenical unity of the Christian Church and its theologians—and thus our presupposed or yet to be won ecumenical unity—is independent of whether or not the authority of the Bible is respected, and that we could discuss in perfect agreement the political and social proclamation of the Bible and yet be of very different minds concerning the meaning of biblical authority. It would make no sense if I were to make light of this business in this way, by leaving off just at the point where this subject confronts us directly. And I need not say that this is honestly not possible for me. Ecumenical unity can thus well be truth or illusion.

If ecumenical unity is an illusion, then quietly and in unruffled tolerance (which we will not then have to owe to each other) let us understand that we are of different minds in this matter of the authority of the Bible: I having my mind, this or that one disagreeing and with a very different mind. Only then I do not know how we would be able to put a common question to the issue of the social and political message of the Bible. If ecumenical unity among us is the truth, then I know of nothing else to say: we must then be in accord in the one Christian faith in our understanding of the authority of the Bible. Precisely from this point must, can, and will it then lead to a fruitful common question about the social and political message of the Bible. I have tried to develop what I understand by being in accord in the one Christian faith in our understanding. I am aware that there are other points of view in this matter.

5

THE CHURCH: THE LIVING CONGREGATION OF THE LIVING LORD JESUS CHRIST[1]

If one wishes to speak of the Christian Church, to understand and describe it, one must always exclusively and consistently hold before one's eyes the living congregation of the living Lord Jesus Christ. If one is of two minds here or stops half way, if one overlooks this reality only the least bit, the profoundest words which might be used on the subject become ambiguous, insipid, and ultimately meaningless. No matter how sincere, all praise of the Church as the Body and Bride of Christ, as the City, Colony, People, and Flock of God then becomes spurious and untrustworthy, for all these New Testament insights and words are related to the living

[1] This is substantially the address which Barth made in 1948 at the Amsterdam Assembly in which the World Council of Churches was established.

congregation of the living Lord Jesus Christ and to it alone. No matter how earnest, all discussion about the nature and unity of the Church, its order and task, its inner life and its commission in the world then leads into uninteresting dead-ends. It is to be feared that no matter how honorable and zealous, all concern about the Church not focused concretely on this reality must ultimately be in vain. Here there is one sign alone in which we can fight with the promise of victory.

In what follows, we will speak of (1) the *essence* of the Church, i.e., its nature and existence; (2) the *threat* to the Church, i.e., the danger of its losing its existence as Church; and (3) that which alone can preserve it from this danger: the *renewal*, or reformation of the Church, on the basis of its origin.

The reality which we have in mind when we use the word "Church" is the living congregation of the living Lord Jesus Christ.

THE ESSENCE OF THE CHURCH

The concept "Church" is a concept of dynamic reality. It speaks of the Lord Jesus Christ risen from the dead and of His congregation which is hurrying from there toward His future self-revelation. This concept speaks of the peculiar *history* between God and man in the time which is determined and characterized by these two dates, one being its beginning, the other its goal. It is in this history that God allows certain men to live as His friends, as witnesses of the reconciliation of the world with Himself which has already taken place in Jesus Christ. It is in this event that God allows these men to be heralds of the victory which He has won over sin, suffering, and death, harbingers of His coming revelation and those who make known the burning love of the Creator for His whole creation. The Church is the community of men which God allows to live under this determination and with this character. In this sense, the time between the resurrection of Jesus Christ and His return is the time of the Church. It is the time of this history of which we have been speaking. This is the time in which the community is gathered together, as an act coming down from heaven, from God's eternal throne and out of the secret of the triune God, and coming forth upon earth, reaching into the creaturely world whose history runs toward its end. The Church exists by *happening*. The Church exists as the *event* of this *gathering together*. This is what we must develop next.

The essence of the Church is the event in which men are placed together before the fact of the reconciliation of the world, which has taken place in Jesus Christ and thus under the condemning grace and the gracious judgment of God, that thereby they may be summoned to give thanks together and to love their neighbor to His praise. In that this peculiar togetherness takes place in the midst of the general history of the world, with its combinations and contradictions, the congregation of Jesus Christ comes into being and endures, the Church exists. Thus and only thus: for those who live together in this community as the recipients of this gift and as bearers of this task are the community of "saints," apart from which there can be no Church in the sense of the New Testament. The word "Church" points to the dynamics of this human event which takes place in the midst of the rest of human history, or else it is an empty word pointing to nothing.

The essence of the Church is the event in which this peculiar human togetherness becomes possible and effectual.

It happens that Jesus Christ gives Himself to these men—to each one individually in his own way, but to each in the same reality—to be known as their Lord, who is also the Lord of the world, the Lord of the world who is also their Lord. It happens that He makes use of His sovereignty not to subjugate these men, but to awaken them to *free obedience*. And it happens that the mutuality of their obedience rests not on the fact that each one is forced or constrained by the others, but on the fact that all of them, directly in the freedom of their subordination to Him who is Lord of them all, find themselves united also in freedom toward each other. The word "Church" must point to this sovereignty of Jesus Christ, and just because of this also to this free community, which is free toward Him and free in the mutual relationship of all its members. Otherwise, this word "Church" points where there is no Church.

The essence of the Church is the event in which God's Word and revelation in Jesus Christ, and the office of Jesus Christ as God's ordained Prophet, Priest, and King, is accomplished to the extent that it becomes a *Word* which is directed toward, reaches, and touches certain men. In this event, these men are touched in such a way that with their human existence they give an answer corresponding to this word. In this event they receive the freedom to make an accounting with their whole being for the truth revealed in Jesus Christ, for His giving of Himself for their and the whole world's sins, for His Lordship as the Resurrected. In short, they receive the freedom to follow Him and in this sense to be "Christians." The Church is distinguished from the world by the fact that for the Church, God's work is not only objectively in progress, but God's work reaches and awakens it both as God's Word and as its human answer. And this community is

78

distinguished from everything which only seems to be a community by the fact that God's work within it is not merely known and acknowledged as a deposited and transmitted truth of faith, but is an event which actually takes place in the historical association of the call of Christ and Christian obedience. The word "Church," if it is to be a genuine word, must refer in every case to this historical association.

To be more concrete about it: The essence of the Church is the event in which the Holy Scriptures as the prophetic-apostolic witness to Jesus Christ carry through the "demonstration of the Spirit and power" (and thus their self-attestation) for particular men, so that these men receive the freedom to know themselves as men enlightened and overcome by this witness, i.e., by Him to whom this witness points. That the Holy Scriptures are kept near at hand and are respected by them as the final authority, that they are expounded among them in preaching, instruction, and pastoral care and applied to their lives, is not the whole story. Rather, what happens among these men is this: the Holy Scriptures speak and are heard as God's Word, the moving rain shower, of which Luther spoke, in fact falls upon this place. Here it becomes true: "He who hears you [the apostles] hears me." And here, in and with all this, the Holy Scriptures establish the Church. It exists and is established there, and only there, where the apostolic witness in fact does not remain hidden, but is seen like the city upon the mountain. There is a fruitful intercourse of the Bible with men and of men with the Bible. The word "Church" must point to this intercourse. It may by no means point elsewhere—not even elsewhere in addition.

The essence of the Church (seen from within) is the event which is called in the New Testament "the fellowship of the

Holy Spirit." The fellowship of the Holy Spirit is nothing other than the actually operative might and power of the work of the Lord Jesus Christ, which has become a word addressed to particular men and has awakened their answer. The fellowship of the Holy Spirit creates the living community. There is no passage in the New Testament on the basis of which the Church might be seen or understood in and of itself, so to speak, or in any other way than as the fellowship of the Holy Spirit, which is given in common to certain men and realized by them together. Again, there is no passage of the New Testament which would allow or incline us to understand the fellowship of the Holy Spirit as anything other than the event which takes place between the living Lord Jesus Christ and certain men, in which His life and suffering, His death and resurrection becomes a divine Word to them, to which they may, must, wish to and can give their human answer. The fellowship of the Holy Spirit is the act proceeding from the very heart of God, in the accomplishment of which it becomes true that certain men in the midst of this world know that which is effective for the whole world but is not yet known to be effective by the rest of the world, which in fact the rest of the world has to be informed of by these men: that Jesus Christ is the Lord. The word "Church" must under all circumstances have as its content the fellowship of the Holy Spirit understood in this way.

This could also be said in another way: The essence of the Church is the event in which the baptism into the name of the triune God, which many men have received in different times, in fact bring to their remembrance that they have been received into the friendship of God and therefore have been made responsible before the whole world for the things of God. And it could also be put this way: The essence of the

Church is the event in which these many men, as often as they have all received the bread and the cup of the Lord's Supper, anticipating the power and joy of the future revelation, share already here and now in the "wedding feast of the Lamb" and therefore already here and now are preserved together and are built up together unto eternal life. The word "Church" denotes the history, the action, the divine giving and the human receiving of baptism and the Lord's Supper. Then and only then is it a meaningful word.

The essence of the Church is the event in which the community is a light shining also in the world. The Church exists in that it becomes visible to the world (whether understood by the world or not) as a living community, living in the sense that it hears and responds to God's Word, stands and delivers as the fellowship of the Holy Spirit, is on the move from baptism and goes toward the Lord's Supper. It is a question of the event in which this community, in the midst of the world, distinguishes itself from the world and thereby inevitably becomes offensive to the world in a particular way. It is a question of this community opening wide its doors and windows in order to truly share not in the fraud and especially not in the religious and moralistic illusions of its environment, but in its real concerns, needs, and tasks, that it may represent a calm center of lodging and reflection in contrast to the world's activity and idleness, and also in order to be, in this context, the source of prophetic unrest, admonition, and instigation, without which this transitory world can never endure. And before all else, this community must be open to the world in order to make visible, with its proclamation of the kingdom of God, the clear, but also severe limits of all human movement and effort, progress and regress, ascents and descents. The Church does not exist by pondering, studying, discussing, and preparing itself for this relationship to the world. The Church exists in actually accomplishing this relationship in each time with the appropriate sense of security, realism, and necessity. The consequence of this is that it may then make the appropriate human response also in this respect to the Word of God spoken to it. The word "Church" must point to this *conduct* of the Church in the world. Otherwise, the word is empty and points to some sort of darkness in which the real Church is not to be found.

Luther seems to have thought for a time of dropping the word "Church" altogether and replacing it with the word *Gemeinde*: congregation, or community. It could have had an immeasurable significance—not alone for the Lutheran Church!—had he carried through with this seriously. The proposal has much to be said for it. The thing which is designated "Church" in the Creed is so concrete that the word which we use for it must under all circumstances be the kind of word which mediates to the hearer or reader a correspondingly concrete picture. The Greek-Latin word *ecclesia* did that originally. The French word *église* certainly does not do this any longer, and the Nordic word *kirche, kerk* (Church), over the meaning of which scholars still fail to agree, definitely does not do it for us today. The word *Gemeinde (congregatio)* expresses, on the contrary, something which is surely still concrete for us now. Yet Luther's proposal does not solve the whole problem. The Greek-Latin word *ecclesia* speaks basically not of the existence or condition of a community or congregation, but of the event of its congregating. So the mere substitution of "congregation" or "community" for the word "Church" would not be worthwhile. What is decisive is that we learn again to think when we use the word "Church" not only of an organization, and when we use the better word "community" not only of the existence and the condition of a society, but with both words, rather on the event of a gathering. It belongs to the very essence of the Church—and nothing with which we have to do in the Church, properly, may be understood apart from this—that the Church is the "event of a gathering together" and in this sense a "living congregation." We have tried to say what the Church is by describing this event itself. Seen in this light, obviously, the much misused adjective "ecclesiastical" would have to be subjected to a more basic critique and revision.

THE THREAT TO THE CHURCH

The Lord Jesus Christ lives, "sitting on the right hand of God, the Father almighty, from whence he will come to judge the living and the dead." In a totally different way, although from Him and with Him, there lives on earth, in the "time-between," in the midst of world history, His congregation. With respect to its Head, the Church is divine in nature and manner. As the Body of that Head, it is without doubt and unequivocally human. In and of itself, it is an element of creaturely and therefore threatened reality. Its existence is an existence secured, unthreatened, and incontestable only from above, only from God, not from below, not from the side of its human members. In the event of God's Word and Spirit, it is secured from danger, justified, sanctified, cleansed, and preserved from evil by the fact that it is from above, from God, and only by this! In its Lord Jesus Christ (but also, only in Him) is its security. From Him (but also, only from Him) does it receive the promise. By looking up to Him (and only thus) it gains confidence in its continuance and stay. Its continuance in time is accomplished in the continuation of its establishment by further demonstrations of the gracious God, in the continuation of the history in which the Holy Scriptures are the active, operative subject (*regina ac magistra*), in new revelations and self-attestations of the divine Word and Spirit. *Perpetuo mansura est*: It will be for all time.[1]

It is God's faithfulness which promises and guarantees this continuance! That and that alone, for from the side of its human members, there is no such guarantee available. Their faith, although awakened by God's Word and Spirit, is not their own inalienable possession which cannot be lost; and that applies also to their knowledge, their obedience, their love, their hope, and their prayer. The possibility of unbelief, false belief, and superstition, of ignorance, indifference, hate, and doubt, even of the powerlessness of their prayer—all lie close at hand and will continue so to lie as long as time lasts, as long as the final revelation of the victory of Jesus Christ has not yet dispersed these shadows. Insofar, the existence of the Church from its human side is a threatened existence. Since God is not yet all in all, it cannot be otherwise. Admittedly the threat to the Church need not be acute, need not become a fall into temptation. In order not to be tempted, it would have to be protected from every threat by its living Lord. But that is just the point: The Church never and nowhere lives in dependence on its living Lord in such a way that the threat under which it exists has no way to get at it, cannot in fact become a temptation. In fact, it is unhappily the case that the threat to the Church is acute at all times and everywhere, that it is not only a threatened, but in one way or another a tempted Church. The community "without spot or wrinkle" (Eph. 5:27) is the community which with Jesus Christ "will

[1] *Augsburg Confession*, VII.

be revealed in glory" (Col. 3:4), never and nowhere the community in the midst of world history rushing toward its end.

The threat and temptation to the Church can have many causes and take many forms. It can be that the light of the divine Word which has placed men in the light and also enlightened them, places them still in the light, and yet now no longer enlightens them, because their eyes have become heavy with sleep. We know what the Gospel says about the watchful servants. Over against them stand the servants who suddenly can only blink, whose open eyes are still sleeping inwardly and who therefore cannot in fact see. They know the Bible and the ancient Creeds, the Confessions of faith, and their catechism. They acknowledge their authority. They nod their heads in earnest faithfulness and say obediently, Yes, Yes! But they have already missed the point, that the old words, yes, the witness of God, are an address directed to them, an address to which they themselves must answer here and now with their own words, with their own lives, in dialogue with the needs and tasks of the present world, as if they had heard it for the first time—as they have indeed heard it for the first time in their situation here and now. The great objective wheel still turns, but already it is turning, unfortunately, in the empty air, for already the little subjective wheel, which should be turned by the other, has become disconnected—a few feeble turns more and it will then stand still. The Christians still stand up and assert their faith, or else the faith of their fathers, and already God's revelation has become for them a world of ghosts full of worthy truths and high moral laws, with which they themselves basically no longer know how to begin, with which they therefore only dare bother the world in a half-hearted way, wearily stifling their own yawns.

———

Jesus Christ as He who is risen from the dead has become for them a religious idea: in Existentialistic Marburg,[1] one can rightly say, He has become a Myth. All that remains of the congregation's expectation of, and hurrying toward, His coming is the activity of a worthy museum keeper and the to-and-fro of a few happenstance-interested museum visitors!

It can also happen—and this is another form of the Church under temptation—that Christians become squint-eyed. We know what the Gospel says (Matt. 6:22) about the healthy eye and about another sort of eye in contrast to this, that the latter is false, and as a result the whole body becomes full of darkness. The light of God's Word shines upon Christians and they see it too. But they also look elsewhere. They have no idea of denying God or being disobedient to Him. Perhaps they want to serve Him with great zeal. But they seek also that which pleases themselves and other men as well as that which pleases God, and they will not entertain the thought that these are two different things. Somewhere along the way, they have fallen in love and become involved with themselves: perhaps in the interests and corresponding morality of their surrounding society, perhaps in just the natural and usual human way it happens in this country or that, perhaps out of a dominant optimism or even pessimism—or, what is yet worse and more dangerous, they may have fallen in love with themselves in the form of their own form of Christendom which has been handed down to them, in the particular honorable forms of faith and worship, in some special form of Christian experience and life, in a particular arrangement of the relationship between Church and state, between Christian and political

---

[1] Rudolf Bultmann was for many years, and at the time when this address was delivered, Professor at the University of Marburg, Germany. Ed.

existence. They speak of "the Word of God" and never notice that they actually mean one of these forms or arrangements. They say "Christian faith" and mean faith in the eternity of this form or arrangement. They say "Christian faithfulness" and mean faithfulness to such an arrangement. On it they now set out to build the Church, and they even suppose they may and must also offer this to the world as "Christianity"!

The worst form of temptation for the Church is that which is described in the Gospel with the picture of the "blind leading the blind" (Matt. 15:14). The eyes of Christians can become blind. They are flooded by the light of the divine Word, but what good does it do them? It no longer reaches them because they are somewhere else: in a self-made world of their own religious dreams. In effect, they have only a memory left of the fact that Jesus Christ was, is, and will be the Lord. The Bible has become for them a source of verbal material for their own thoughts. And their own thoughts proceed from the premise that the religious man is his own Lord: God's Law is the ideal which he lays down for himself, the Gospel is the aid with which he comforts himself, sancti-fication is the discipline which he imposes upon himself, the kingdom of God is the "brave new world" which he can and will build for himself. The Church has itself become the world, in a certain sense the prophet of the world, its proc-lamation is of man who has become God, of flesh that has become the Word. And still they have not noticed that they have thereby become nothing and completely meaningless for those about them.

These are a few of the forms of the threatened Church which is actually fallen into temptation. It then happens, clearly, in each form in its own way, that the event which has its origin in the living Lord Jesus Christ comes to a standstill in the congregation, and the life of the congregation, which corresponds to this event, has no continuance. There is no necessity about this continuance. The congregation stands in danger. The congregation consists of men who are able to sin against God's grace. It is indeed a miracle when that does not happen, and this miracle can, but it does not have to happen. The Church is not infallible. Human freedom, which should correspond to the sovereignty of Jesus Christ, can fail. Man's natural closeness with respect to God can ever again become visible, now in its worst, now in its "Christian" form. The answer which Christians owe God's Word can remain unspoken. The ears which hear the witness of Scripture can become deaf. The fellowship of the Holy Spirit can be squandered away, baptism and the Lord's Supper become empty signs, the proclamation of the Church to the world a painful subject to be discussed. The history which is opened up from the side of the divine Subject can come to a standstill in the human subject. All this *can* happen. The past history of the Church and the contemporary news of the Church documents that all this does happen, and just how it happens.

Now where this event comes to a halt and ceases to be an event, *there the Church ceases to be the Church*. It is a sign of God's patience that this does not necessarily need to be the case immediately and all along the line, and that the current of life between the Lord and His congregation is broken only partially, only in certain aspects and areas of its existence. But let no man be deceived about this: where and insofar as it is broken, where and insofar as that event is no longer something which happens, there the Church ceases to be the Church, there something else, which only in a false, improper way can be called "Church," steps into its place. "You have the name of being alive, and you are dead" (Rev. 3:1). And it is dangerous when the Church is only partly dead, partly no longer the Church. This part is then a cancer that can easily eat into sound tissue and be the death of the whole body. Then the borderline case threatens that the whole Church will cease to be the Church. If that does not happen, then it is only because the living Lord Jesus Christ cannot die and because the Church is on its way to the resurrection that depends on Him. In and of itself, the Church could otherwise only decay and perish.

When the Church dies, the horizon does not become clear, of course: a simple vacuum is not the result. It pertains to the darkness of the threat and temptation which besets the Church (or seen in another light, of course, it is a sign of God's patience) that something which seems to be and look like the Church, though not deserving that name, remains on the scene. Even a dead congregation, or the dead element of a living congregation, is accustomed to have the form of "Church," "Church" tradition, and "Church" life. Just as all these cannot prevent the threatening and tempting of the Church, so as a rule the worst temptation of the Church will not exclude these. In fact it can even happen that the Church might cease to be the Church and that then the thing which is still called "Church" really comes to life and gains might, splendor, and significance in world history. It can happen that precisely the apparition of the Church or the apparent Church, the Church with the sleepy, squinting, or blind eyes, the Church in which the confrontation of God with men and of men with God is no longer an event, but only an institution, dogma, program, and problem, can fall on especially good days in this age and may enjoy the special respect of society and the state. If the Church falls on such good days, then it has indeed cause to ask itself whether it might not be the Devil whom it should acknowledge and thank for the fact that it has long since become the apparent Church. But the other question is also not to be silenced: whether, when bad days come, it might not be God's well-earned judgment which sooner or later must meet it already in this age, since it has become only the apparent Church.

That the threat to the Church is acute, that in the name of the Church there are many dead and apparent churches, is decisively indicated by the fact that its unity is problematic. Under the living Lord Jesus Christ there can be only *one* living Christian congregation: each particular Christian congregation and every grouping of the same in all their differences will know all these as only different forms of the *one* congregation, in which each will recognize itself in the others and the others in itself. The essence of the Church in the event of the divine Word and its human response is a single essence which is not divisible, separable, and which contains no inner contradictions. But it is just this essence of the Church in this event, in the uninterrupted current of its connection with the living Lord, which is the *one and only* guarantee of its unity. Should this event come to a standstill, should the Church try to be the Church other than in the happening of this event, should its eyes become sleepy, squinting, or blind, should it become an apparent Church, then its unity must be lost immediately. He who gathers it together is the living Lord. A ghost world of objective truths and high moral laws will not assemble the Church, nor will any of those combinations of things pleasing to God and things pleasing to men, and certainly no more will any of those dream pictures with which men glorify themselves under the name of God. Dead congregations can only be divided congregations, only falsely united in such a way that at any minute they might be in open conflict with each other. But the matter is yet more serious: the fact that living and dead congregations live together more or less in peace in no way suggests that they might become a single congregation.

If there are any two things which separate like fire and water, they are the living and the dead congregations, the Church and the apparent Church.[1] The work of proclamation and pastoral care (but on the basis of the confession of the truth and thus the assertion of the contradiction) will of course not only be possible there. They will be necessary and commanded. But unity (as long as reality does not replace appearance or death give way to new life) will be completely impossible. Love which does not burn in this connection, love which would seek another, more comfortable unity than that which has been lost and is to be found in Jesus Christ Himself, would not be Christian love, nor would it create unity. It could only make the living one of these two congregations itself a dead congregation. But the fact remains that the unity of the Church is torn by the existence of the apparent Church. The fact is worth pondering, that the living congregation suffers because of this situation not only subjectively but, in that it does its duty (as it goes its own proper way) to overcome the apparent Church, it will also suffer objectively. The living congregation is itself not infallible nor beyond danger, and its own danger will undoubtedly become greater by the fact that it has this dead congregation, this apparent Church next to it and cannot exist otherwise than in contradiction to it. This means the temptation for it to conform to this other where it

---

[1] The rest of this paragraph is clarified by recalling the tensions existing between the Confessing Church and the so-called "German Christians" who co-operated with the Nazi government under Hitler.

ought not. It also means the temptation for it to become presumptuous and callous where it ought not, the temptation to live on the basis of ecclesiastical opposition, as though this were the source of the revelation which fed it. This is the temptation of ecclesiastical self-righteousness, the realization of which would mean the death of this congregation, its transformation into an apparent Church. There has never been a living congregation which has not had to fight this double temptation as soon as it was face to face with a dead congregation. The questionable character of the unity of the Church, arising from the threat under which the Church lives, therefore, is really more than an aesthetic lack. The division of the Church is not only an aspect, therefore, of that which threatens it; rather, the threat lies essentially in this division. Therefore, the question about the preservation and about the renewal of the Church must be ultimately the question about its unity.

THE RENEWAL OF THE CHURCH

The Church is threatened. Therefore it needs to be preserved. Preservation of the Church, however, must clearly mean: renewal of its essence as event, renewal of its foundation, renewal of its being gathered together as congregation. Since the actually acute threat to the Church in its parts and in the whole is a matter of the existence or nonexistence of the Church, anything less than renewal, any mere support, aid, improvement, or the like will not suffice for its preservation. If the Church is preserved, if in spite of all it has continuance in time, then that must mean that it experiences anew, again and again, the same thing which it experienced in coming into existence, an eternally new *reformation* which corresponds to its formation. If the Church is not caught up in reformation, then it has fallen into temptation, fallen headlong into being non-Church, and so fallen beyond rescue.

Preservation, and therefore renewal, and therefore reformation of the Church, however, can come only from its living Lord. The congregation threatened with death can be protected from death only by Him. The congregation which is already dead can be awakened from the dead to new life and be rescued only by Him. The hope and the only hope of the Church is that He so speak His Word that the corresponding answer is found among Christians, that He accept and make use of the witness of His apostles once again, that He make the exposition and application of this witness strong, deep, and contemporary in laying hold of men, both for the Christians themselves and also for the world, that He operate as Lord of the covenant of baptism, that in the Lord's Supper He come and be our guest, that what He has given us be blessed. No sure hope can be placed in good will, religious sincerity, or in Christian ideals. All this is exposed to temptation and already fallen. All this is the completely human realm of the Church and needs renewal. It can never be the source of its own renewal. He, Jesus Christ, who stands under no threat and needs no renewal, He, the Lord, is the hope of the Church.

He—He alone—is its hope. That is what the Church has to express in its polity, to which we now turn in this connection. The polity of the Church must in any case be so formed that it present the least possible resistance to the renewal of the Church by its living Lord, and guarantee humanly speaking the maximum degree of being open, free, and at the disposal of Him and the reformation which He accomplishes. What else can polity do? No polity can create renewal or reformation. But this it can and must do—and therefore this must be kept in mind by Christians in their division when the polity and constitution of the Church is the problem before them: the polity of the Church can and must give a form to the Church which expresses the conviction that Jesus Christ alone is its hope.

The one, holy, universal, apostolic Church exists as a *visible congregation*, the visible congregation which is assembled by God's Word, comforted and exhorted by God's Word, and which serves God's Word in the world. That is what the polity of the Church has to express first of all. The Church does not exist as the *invisible* and thus amorphous sum of all the "faithful" then alive. It is not this because such a *civitas platonica* can never represent the acting and responsible living congregation before its living Lord. Moreover, the Church surely does not exist in the individuals who have gathered together of their own choice (according to a poor conception of "democracy") or in the majority of such individuals. It is not this because the call of Jesus Christ to all men to believe is what establishes believers among them as the Church, and not vice versa. And the Church also does not exist as an ordained representation of Jesus Christ to the congregation, or of the congregation to Jesus Christ, in so-called "orders" regardless of whether one means the order of pastor or the order of presbyter. The Church exists even less in any sort of authority over the congregation in the office of a bishop or in a hierarchy, and it also does not exist in the representatives of these representatives of the congregations sitting together in synod or in a hierarchy of such synods or in their executive committees, not to speak of some "consistory," "High Consistory" or the like, set up over the congregations by some outside agency, in keeping with certain (bad) political practices—and that also applies to instances when these are called a "council of the brethren."[1] It is not any of these because all such inter-positions of human sovereignty and authority can only hinder and not further the free operation of God's Word and Spirit.

The living Lord Jesus Christ is concerned directly with His living congregation, not indirectly, not through this or that system of representation, not by way of some successive appeal, thought out by man. "You know that the rulers of the people dominate them and the great men (namely, the evil ones!) exercise power over them. It shall not be thus among you" (Matt. 20:25). The fear which stands behind the idea of all authoritarian Church structure is not a good counselor. Such fear is accustomed to give way before all sorts of human arbitrariness. Is it not really the fear that without this inter-position, the living Lord might have too little—or perhaps too much—power in the living congregation? But if this fear is forbidden, then there is no reason to evade the simple prop-osition: the Church is there and only there "where two or three are gathered together in my name" (Matt. 18:20) and therefore in the visible congregation, visible to itself and to others. Here it will be believed or else it will not be believed at all. Here it lives or else it does not live at all. An ecclesiastical polity which is not derived from observing the congregation and from the concept of congregation is not worthy of the name. It can only be false polity, disorder rather than order, and therefore it can only establish disaster: and it will do this all the more when it is all the more consistently and thor-oughly derived from some other point.

[1] The reference is to various forms of ecclesiastical administration in recent German history, Ed.

The word "congregation" does not necessarily and exclusively have to mean *local congregation* as the gathering of Christians of a particular local area. There is no reason why the "two or three" might not be gathered together under some other aspect than that of locality. This point will be of importance for us in a moment. But the simplest, most available, and insofar exemplary and regular form of such a gathering is in fact the local congregation, the boundary of which coincides with those of some residential community. It is constituted thus by the possibility of regular services of worship.

What is worship? "Liturgy" means the proclamation of the mighty acts of God by which the congregation is established and in the celebration of which it permits itself to be established anew, again and again. By participation in this worship—to which belong in the broad sense also the instruction of youth, brotherly discipline, pastoral and other forms of care—and from this worship, built upon it and active in it, the Christian congregation lives, its members serve each other and together serve their Lord, and with their witness serve the world. Congregation means fellowship in prayer and confession, in the action of baptism and Lord's Supper, mutual reception of, and mutual exertion in, the Gospel proclamation. The congregation lives in this concrete event, in its presuppositions and its consequences. In general, but not necessarily, that will mean: it lives as a local community. By living as such, there has been done what can be done from the human side, so that at least no stone is placed in the way of its renewal by its Lord.

In that it lives as such a congregation, it will become evident that the one gift and task given it by its Lord has different forms in its many members, and that it therefore may and must offer different services in its service of worship. Let us speak of services and not of offices! When the different services are acknowledged, then there can be congregational service and the whole congregation arises and endures. In the living congregation, it is axiomatic that no member may be without such a service. That is how little this question of service has to do with "authorities" established from above or elected from beneath! There simply are no ecclesiastical "authorities" in the congregation except the Word of God in its biblical witness, and it is served by the whole congregation in all of its services. Reaching a consensus in the congregation about the aptitude of this or that member for this or that service to the Word—that is what "Church elections" are.

There is a particular "servant of the Word" who, in the framework of his particular form of the gift and task which is given to all, helps make the worship of the whole congregation, and so the congregation itself, the existence of the Church on its human side, possible and real. But there can follow from this no idea whatsoever of one service over or under other services: it is a matter of difference of function. The minister is not placed above the other elders, nor the bellringer beneath the professor of theology. There is no room here for the distinction of "clergy" and "laity" or for a merely "learning" or "listening" Church because there is no member of the Church who is not in his own place all of this. Let it be said to the congregations again: it is they unconditionally and in all of their members, it is they, in the full meaning of the concept "Church" and as such, who are called into action. The preservation and thus the renewal of the Church depends on the congregations becoming real congregations. That is humanly speaking. We do not forget that the renewal of the Church can happen only as an event coming from its Lord and

Head. But when this happens among men, then certainly as the decisive basis for all else, this is what happens: there takes place no conference of bishops or other "Churchmen"; no gathering of ministerial groups conspire; no dictates are handed down by an authority or Consistory; but instead, the congregation simply *becomes the congregation*, first of all and as a rule, as a local congregation.

But these local congregations can surely not be the sole form of the one, holy, universal, apostolic Church, because the question of their unity, which is answered internally by the fellowship in worship and in the special services belonging to this, is repeated externally with respect to the relationship of the different local congregations to each other. If each of them is itself, in the full sense of the word, *the* Church, it must follow that they know and acknowledge each other mutually in their indirect identity, and mutually support, advise, help, and to this extent guide each other in their existence and therefore in the renewal and reformation of their existence. In this context, to guide means to serve, not to dominate. Had the congregation in Rome wanted to serve rather than rule, rather than needlessly underscoring its domination, in addition, by erecting a throne in its midst and raising up its incumbent as an infallible judge over the faith and life of all the congregations, we might all be Roman.

Certainly there are organs for the guidance of many congregations: organs which could be thought of at most as summing up in a single ecumenical organ the guidance of every Christian congregation, reflecting the unity of the Lord Jesus Christ in the unity of his biblical witness. But there is no congregation which could stand as the "authority" over the other congregations, even less some ruling bishop or episcopal council, synod, or executive committee, not to speak of some "governing" consistory or the like. The organ of guidance for many or all congregations could only be itself a congregation: a synodal congregation established *ad hoc* out of certain members of the individual congregations involved. It would have to be constituted with respect to its particular purpose—one might even dare to use the expression "as mother congregation"! Its action in the midst of the rest of the congregations would also have to have the consistent character of a particular service of God. In no sense would it be its task to rule over the other congregations, to have them at its disposal. It would not infringe on their freedom in Jesus Christ. Rather, it would strengthen them, speak as *one* congregation to the others, and stand by them in service. It would have the task, however, to proclaim to them the Word of God with respect to the matter of their unity and thus with respect to the fellowship of the saints among them. It would guarantee to them their "catholic," their "ecumenical" character.

In the spiritual authority of the Word of God, it would have to advise them in this particular respect, encourage and also warn and reprove them, call them to take the initiative here and to hold back there, remember the good tradition here and the necessary improvements there. It would serve to co-ordinate them. But in all this, it would work with the congregations as a congregation. It would help them to establish spiritual order and to make it valid. "Church government"? No! Church leadership by such special synodal congregations built up out of the congregations for the congregations? Yes! Congregations in this special service of the Church, exercised with respect to all the other congregations, and thus truly universal? Yes! Congregations which ask in faith about the obedience of faith of the other congregations? Yes! The Holy

Spirit has a governing authority which is matchless. One has only to allow Him to run His course instead of hindering Him. And precisely in order for Him to run His course in every congregation, it is necessary that the leading, synodal entity be itself a free congregation working in freedom, like all the others, standing alongside them and in just this way standing up and answering for them all.

Aside from the synodal congregation, there are other organized cross-connections between the individual local congregations, which are therefore other representations and organs of their unity. Free work-communities come to mind, such as the different youth groups, mission societies, diaconesses, and other special institution and house communities. The military congregations come also to mind, and why should there not also be, in all freedom and honor (not in opposition to the unity of the congregation, but in confirmation of it) from time to time communities of particular Christian intention and tendency? Let us call it by name at once. These special communities of work, which have become necessary and been realized from out of many congregations, and within many congregations have always felt themselves to be and *de facto* have been some sort of congregation in the service of God. They may and should do so in all seriousness *de jure*. They should in no way evade the claim and the responsibility of being in fact congregations, whether large or small, conducting worship, thinking and acting in the service of God and therefore in their particular form, being also the one, holy, universal, and apostolic Church. They are no more merely associations, groups, circles, or parties than the leadership of the Church are merely officials. They too stand each on its own spot in the service of the gift and task given to the whole living congregation of the living Lord

Jesus Christ, and in consort with the local congregations and with the synodal congregation in the service of their one common commission. If they exist by knowing and wanting this, if they exist in the exercise of this service, then they are also the Church in the full meaning of the word.

With these basic suggestions, we find ourselves turned back to the beginning of this last reflection. Church polity is no end in itself. The Church is not an end in itself and so neither are the things which pertain to it. That does not mean, however, that the question of polity may be answered in line with nationally, regionally, locally, politically, or socially determined caprice, or in blind adherence to any "confessional stand" of the Fathers in some distant century. The Church's polity, no less than the preaching and confession of the Church, must be shaped root and branch in correspondence to the Word of God. This does not mean the nonsense that it must be taken word for word out of the Bible. But it does mean that this has to be kept in mind: It is a question of the congregation being ready, open, and free for God's Word and for the renewal of the Church by God's Word. With respect to the acute threat to the Church, it is a question of finding the most effective, cleverest, and boldest action, that the direct confrontation and fellowship of the living Lord Jesus Christ with His congregation may again happen as an event, that the broken circuit be again closed, that the history of the waiting and hastening friends of God which has come to a stop might go forward, and the witnesses, proclaimers, and heralds of Jesus Christ again take to the road. That this forward movement really begins lies not within human hands. But it does lie within human hands that the things which hinder it be put out of the way. And here is where the question of the Church's polity enters.

Against the papal form, and also against the episcopal and presbyterian synodal forms of constitution, there is this basic objection, that they not only do not serve the readiness, openness, and freedom of the congregation for the Word of God and therefore for the reformation of the Church; they actually hinder it. They all rest on the remarkable contradiction that they entrust *too little* to men—namely, to the men gathered as Christians to be the living congregation of the Lord Jesus Christ—yet, on the other hand, they entrust too much to men—namely, to those particular office bearers and representatives chosen and ordained by men, entrusted to be representatives within and without the congregation. In one place these forms cannot be too careful to guard against human arbitrariness, in order in the other place to carelessly give it a free hand. Where the former care and the latter carelessness are in effect, there can be no room for the renewal of the Church. Where the polity of the Church is grounded in the former carefulness and the latter carelessness, it can only create new disorder. Why may not the constitution of the Church be at last based on the knowledge that the Church is wholly from God and must await *everything* from Him? These other polities are all open to the charge that they smell a bit of unbelief. How is it possible with them for that history which constitutes the essence of the Christian Church to move forward? All these roads have today come to their end. The discussions between their representatives have long since become sterile. All that remain as possibilities in their context are restorations, not reformations. And for the political recovery so necessary in every country today, a Church built according to these plans has nothing essential to contribute. A Church which was in all its forms a living congregation would be already, in its exemplary existence in the midst of the political structure, a proclamation also in the political realm. But how can it have and be such a proclamation as long as the basis of its polity is contempt of the congregation and anxiety at the thought of its freedom?

The other way, which we have glanced at, is also not a completely new way. It showed itself quite clearly in its basic lines already in the sixteenth and seventeenth centuries in an ecclesiastical movement in England, a movement which until now has been too little noticed or too quickly rejected. The congregations which dared in that time and place to let themselves be formed by this movement made themselves noteworthy at any rate in the critical eighteenth century by having been able to make a far better stand in the face of the Enlightenment, strange as it may seem, than the other English churches, which were apparently so much better armed with their episcopal or presbyterian synodal authority. It was from these congregations that the "Pilgrim Fathers" derived. From the free spirit with which they built the Church in America, it can hardly be said that they lacked organizing strength. And it is scarcely an arbitrary construction on the matter, adding to this with good reason the well-known political health and maturity of Englishmen in general, that there for centuries have been just such Christian congregations. The inner necessity of their way need only be more deeply grounded, their ecumenical validity and significance need only be set more sharply in the light and more consequentially and at the same time more circumspectly argued than has been the case up till now. Their problems are true problems: true, because they force us to reflect on that which is central for the Christian Church. It is no accident that this movement has been taken up again in our time by a group of young English theologians under a wholly new perspective, not unrelated to the development of Continental Protestant theology and the ecumenical movement.[1] And it is also no accident that the so-called Younger Churches, in what was once the "mission field," have clearly set forth in this same direction, on their own and without seeing themselves driven by any connection with the former tradition. "Who knows," wrote Friedrich Loofs as far back as 1901, (at that time thinking particularly of the German situation) "whether it might not be the case one day, when the established Churches of the old world collapse, that the congregational form of Church may yet have a future also among us?" That may have been a truly prophetic "who knows?"

---

[1] Possibly refers to the circle out of which came *The Catholicity of Protestantism, being a report presented to His Grace the Archbishop of Canterbury by a group of Free Churchmen*, edited by R. Newton Flew and Rupert E. Davies (London: Lutterworth Press, 1950). Ed.

6

CHRISTIAN ETHICS

Ethics is the attempt to give a human answer to the question of the dignity, correctness, and excellence of human activity. Christian ethics is thus primarily the attempt to give this answer as it is made by those who confess themselves to be Christian and who wish with more or less seriousness to be Christians. Because this attempt has been undertaken from the beginning and everywhere where there have been Christians, Christian ethics must be understood as a phenomenon of spiritual and cultural life, as part of the history of peoples and nations. But since all the attempts to find an answer to the question of the excellence of human activity, Christian included, are and must be debatable, Christian ethics is also to be understood as a specific field of the critical theological discipline in which the correctness of the answers to this question which have arisen in history is to be tested.

I would like to sketch with quick strokes what the subject

---

matter is in this area, i.e., how the question about the dignity of human activity has at heart always been answered by Christians, and how it must at heart always be answered under all circumstances.

Christian ethics is, like all ethics, an attempt to give a human answer to this question. But its answer does not belong among that group of answers which man himself can give and is accustomed to give, on the basis of his reason, his conscience, or on the basis of his knowledge of nature and history. Christian ethics is an answer in a singular and pregnant sense of the word. Christian ethics answers the call from God which has gone forth to man, goes forth now, and will go forth again. "You have been told, O man, what is good." Christian ethics is the attempt to repeat what has been said to man, to repeat in human words and with human concepts the divine commandment. Christian ethics rests upon the attentiveness and openness of man for God's commandment, for God's own answer to the question about the good, and to this extent, for the divine ethic.

Christian ethics does not rest, therefore, on a philosophy or Weltanschauung and it does not consist of the development of an idea or a principle or a program. Man answers the question about the good with these sorts of answers when he is locked in a conversation with himself. Christian ethics is not part of this conversation which man carries on with himself. Christian ethics begins, therefore, not with what might be called reflection. It begins with hearing. Christian ethics thinks through that which God has already thought about human activity, and Christian ethics repeats what has already been said to man about his activity. It must always be the case, therefore, that Christian ethics takes its point of departure from what must be a puzzle for him who is not yet or perhaps no longer prepared to listen to God. Such a one must always be baffled by the question of whence Christian ethics derives its concepts, how it uses them, and how the same concepts have such a different meaning and effect here from their meaning and effect elsewhere. He who would understand Christian ethics may not evade having to take his stand at least hypothetically on the strange spot from which it thinks and speaks, where man must always first of all hear, listen to God's Word, and only then think and speak.

Christian ethics is connected with a history between God and man which has taken place, still takes place, and will take place in the future. More specifically, it has to do with the active role of man in this history. God does something and does it in such a way that man is thereby called to do something in turn. This call of God to man, which goes forth in this history, is God's command. It is the divine ethic, which Christian ethics seeks in its human way to understand and present. That which forms the subject matter, in relation to this history and this call to man, can perhaps be first of all understood by comparison with the system of modern Socialism or Communism. This system consists of a concept of a line of development which runs through human history: the history of the development of the economy, ownership, and work, from which there breaks forth, according to Socialist-Communist teaching, a quite particular call, word, and imperative to contemporary man. But however significant and true may be the history of ownership and work, it is but child's play compared to the history to which Christian ethics is related. And however powerfully the Socialist-Communist call may sound, it is but a small whisper compared to the call which Christian ethics has to repeat, understand, and present.

Of just what sort is this history? What sort of a drama is

this, of which the English author Dorothy Sayers can say that it was the greatest drama ever played?

To say it with the simplest words possible: God became, was, and is a man. And it happened that God as this man was not a success, but had to suffer and died as a condemned criminal on the gallows. And it happened, further, that this man who was God was raised from the dead. But thereby it happened that every man in Him and all men by Him were exalted to the glory of God. I anticipate. The conclusion of this history consists in this: that it will happen, it will be revealed for all and to all, that our guilt and need is taken away by the person of this man, and that we are called in the person of this man to the glory of God. Thus it happened, and therein happened that God was and is and will be gracious to us. That is the history between God and man, the history of Jesus Christ, God's covenant and mercy. It is to this history that Christian ethics is related.

Christian ethics is the fruit that grows on this tree. Christian ethics cannot be understood if this story is omitted or mis-interpreted. For it is just this history which calls out continu-ally to the activity of men. This history concerns man, indeed man as he lives in action. This history is the word which calls for man's answer, which he must give with his actions. Jesus Christ calls man to discipleship, i.e., to a human life in the freedom which He gives.

We have now come far enough for me to give, in the most general and simple terms, an answer to the question about the Christian meaning of the good activity of men. What is "good" in the Christian sense of the word? Good, in the Christian sense, is that conduct and action of man's which corresponds to the conduct and action of God in this history. That human work is good, therefore, in which man accepts—

and not only accepts but affirms—that God humbled Himself for him in order that man might live and rejoice. That activity of man is good, in the Christian sense, in which man acknowledges that he stands in need of this divine mercy; yet that he is not only in need of it, but also shares in it. To say it briefly: That action of man's is good in which man is thankful for God's grace. Nothing else? No, nothing else. For everything else which might be called good, faith, love, hope, every thankful good virtue and duty, is contained in this one: that man be thankful for God's grace. You know the passage in the Gospel: "You are to be perfect as your heavenly Father is perfect" (Matt. 5:48). The perfection of God, however, is that which He demonstrates in this history, the perfection of His grace. That human conduct and act of man's is good, therefore, which corresponds to the grace of God.

What then is evil, in the Christian sense of the word? Evil is that conduct and act of man's in which he contradicts the content and the action of God's history, in which he hurries or sneaks past the suffering and the joy of Jesus Christ. That deed of man's is evil in which man, openly or in secret, because of anxiety or pride, is unthankful. That is what is evil. Nothing else? No, nothing else, for everything which is evil from Adam to our own day, from the great horrors of world history down to the little lies and acts of unfriendliness with which we have mutually poisoned our lives, springs from human hate of God's grace.

I would like now to answer a few related questions.

1. What is the meaning of "conscience" in Christian ethics? Very simply it means that we may know what God has done for us. And we may therefore also know about ourselves, and know about ourselves as God knows about us, in order that we might then, on the basis of this knowledge, so choose

and determine ourselves and our acts as God has chosen and determined us. Good or evil action is simply being obedient or disobedient to this knowledge of ours about God and ourselves.

2. What is the significance of the Bible for Christian ethics? The answer to this is not that the Bible is some sort of law book for Christian ethics. It is true that every word, every sentence, and every page of the Bible is important for Christian ethics, but important because they are the documents, the indispensable documents, by means of which we are able again and again to call to remembrance the history of the covenant and the mercy of God, the history of Jesus Christ. In addition, the Bible is the document of that condition of life which is created among men by the grace of God, described, for example, in the Ten Commandments, the Sermon on the Mount, and the admonitions of the apostles. From the Bible one learns to submit to such a condition of life.

3. What is the posture of Christian ethics to the world of human morals? That is, what is its posture to the customs and practices, old and new, to the traditional or perhaps revolutionary rules of life in which man, apparently independent of that history of which we have been speaking, thinks he knows and does "the good"? The answer to this is: Christian ethics runs through this whole world of morals, tests everything and preserves the best, only the best, and that means those things by which from time to time God's grace is best praised. It is surely inevitable that Christian ethics will constantly surprise man and his moral standards again and again.

But now I would like to try to indicate in outline how the history between God and man calls for a continuation in

110

man's activity, how the Word which God speaks to us in that history longs for an answer, how Jesus Christ calls men to discipleship. Thereby I can also indicate how Christian ethics tries to repeat this divine summons.

1. We said that in this history God became man and therefore espoused man's cause, thereby defining man and making Himself man's neighbor for man's sake, His good Samaritan, so that He might have mercy on man as His true neighbor. What does this history say to us? It says: "Go and do likewise." Christian ethics repeats this appeal to mankind. According to Christian ethics, man as such, every man, has a legitimate claim to be seen, affirmed, and accepted. Christian ethics is not neutral. It is not interested in some mighty It, no matter how lofty. Rather, it is concerned wholly and solely with I and Thou. For Christian ethics (and here Immanuel Kant spoke as a Christian), man can never be a means to an end. He is the end himself, the final end. Because he is a man he is honorable, more important than the most glorious thing. Why? Because man is such a good and glorious being? No, but rather because God so honored and dignified him by becoming Himself one of his kind.

2. In this history of which we have spoken, man is rescued by grace alone by the intervention of God for him. What does this history say to us? It says: "Set your mind not on high things, but condescend to the lowly." Christian ethics repeats to itself and to others this summons to sobriety. Christian ethics is not optimistic. It sees man as he is: gone astray, condemned, and lost. It sees him as a being who can only stumble deeper and deeper into corruption, weighed down with illusions and all sorts of reflections. Christian ethics knows that man lives alone by the fact of God's waiting upon man, God's patience and forgiveness. It knows that man

cannot live except by also waiting, having patience, receiving forgiveness, and in turn forgiving others.

3. In this history, man is saved by God's intervention on his behalf. What does that say? It says: "Do not destroy that for which Christ has died." Christian ethics repeats this commission to trust man (who is preserved by God). Christian ethics is not pessimistic. There is no reason to doubt ourselves or others, no reason to hate or despise each other, no reason why we should be unconcerned for each other. Indeed, we all live from the fact that in truth God has arisen on our behalf. And that means hope for each of us, ourselves and the others. "You can, for you should," said Immanuel Kant. "You can, for you may," says Christian ethics.

4. In this history, the one Lord, not to be confused with any other, came to the help of man. "I am God almighty; walk in my paths and be godly." Christian ethics repeats this summons to responsibility on the basis of personal election and calling. Christian ethics is not collective. That is, Christian ethics understands all truly human existence as taking place in man's own free decision and as his own free posture, which does not allow the individual to be bound by any prior decision of some higher authority or by the will of the mass to which he belongs. Obedience in the meaning of Christian ethics takes place always in the solitude of one man before the one God.

5. That which took place in this history was the activity of the mercy of the one God, which touches every man. What does this history say to us? It says: "You are all brothers." Christian ethics repeats this summons to community on the basis of men's common need and the help which is common to all. Christian ethics is not individualistic. Christian ethics shapes community, the community of Christians, first of all,

the community of those who have heard this call. But Christian ethics cannot allow men outside the community of Christians to cut themselves off or construct some sort of party. It can only form community also outside: the civil community. Whether Christian or citizen, man is called by Christian ethics under every circumstance to become involved on the side of the common work in which there can be no opposition, but only co-workers of various persuasions.

6. In this history, God's glory is demonstrated in that God made Himself the slave of man. What does this story say? It says: "He who is the greatest among you is the slave of all." And Christian ethics in its entirety repeats this summons to service. Christian ethics is not aristocratic, knows no royalty, no sovereignty of leader or master other than that which consists in a man being at the disposal of other men, as one link in a chain, as a Christian among Christians, a brother among brothers. (This is the highest dignity of man, that he is called to intercede ever again for the others before God and for God before the others and to clothe this highest dignity in deepest modesty.)

7. God's act for man is inclusive and definitive. "You shall love the Lord your God with your whole heart, your whole soul, your whole mind and all your strength." That is what this history says to us. And Christian ethics repeats this summons to wholeness. (The Christian imperative runs: Expect everything from God, and from God everything.) Christian ethics is in no sense dualistic. It allows no split or separation, no glance into a present without a beyond, and no glance into a beyond without seeing its light shining into the present. It allows no talk of prayer which does not of itself lead into work, and no talk of work which is not grounded in prayer. It knows no soul apart from body, nor a body apart

from soul, no private sphere without public responsibility, and no public responsibility without the quiet pole of privacy. Christian ethics has to do with man, who is wholly lost, wholly rescued and therefore is claimed as a whole man.

That, in a few lines, is the continuation of this history, the discipleship of Jesus Christ, and that is how Christian ethics repeats the divine summons.

Let me sum it up: Christian ethics is clear, meaningful, and realistic in that it stands in this context—i.e., in that it looks back upon this history of which we have spoken. Christian ethics can be understood only from that point. From the other side, this is also true of Christian dogmatics. It also is real and meaningful only as it looks ahead to the man who is called to action by this history. How else were Christian dogmatics, the catechism, and the Creed to be understood, if not together with this summons?

In this context I have tried to define Christian ethics: Christian work is the fruit of Christian faith, Christian law is the form of the Christian gospel, and Christian ethics is the imperative of the indicative of Christian dogmatics. He who would understand the meaning of Christian ethics must take care at all costs to avoid a separation here.

I conclude with a word of the Apostle Paul from his second letter to the Corinthians (5:19–20): "For God was in Christ reconciling the world to Himself, not reckoning to them their sins, and has delivered to us the word of reconciliation. So we are but Christ's ambassadors, for God exhorts you by means of us. So now on behalf of Christ we ask of you: Let yourselves be reconciled with God." That is the whole of Christian ethics.

7

HUMANISM[1]

One of the good things that can be said about the international conference on humanism held in Geneva in 1949 is this: it took a "human" turn. The philosophers and historians, orientalists and natural scientists, theologians and Marxists who gathered there from all over Europe talked together openly, clearly, obligingly and not without humor, not only in public, but also privately around a table. And more than that, they tried to listen to each other and to understand one another as best they could. If "humanism" can also mean that this sort of encounter is possible, then we need not be ashamed of our meeting in Geneva before Socrates, Goethe, or any other of the great men of history whom we are accustomed to call "humanists." How we waited together on our

[1] This chapter contains Barth's reflections on the Geneva conference on "A New Humanism," at which he delivered the address that forms Chapter 1 of this book. Ed.

last day upon the shades of Madame de Staël in the castle at Coppet![2] In such an inhuman era as ours, the success of so human a gathering must surely count as a certain accomplishment.

But of course the picture can be painted in another and sterner way: for the cause of "a new humanism," what was the *outcome* of this meeting? Was it visible in any sort of *rapprochement*? Was it even to be detected in any kind of result? If someone were to ask this question, it could be said in reply that tangible results should not have been expected from an academic meeting of this kind. But the negative fact remains: a gathering, neither small nor exclusive, of European intellectuals of all kinds and persuasions studied and discussed the question of a new humanism for ten days with no other result than a bit of mutual edification and stimulation. No vision appeared from any quarter which might have enlightened and convinced all those who participated, not to speak of a vision which might have been tangibly helpful for the contemporary world. We shall not even mention practical suggestions. Almost every one of us there, insofar as he believed in such a thing, had his own ideas of "the new humanism." And finally, we could not even agree whether a new humanism was to be expected in our time, or only to be desired.

And now the worst: at that conference in Geneva it was apparent (and it was clearer on the tenth day than on the first) that even the *concept* of humanism and its definition were

[2] The country house about ten miles north of Geneva to which Madame de Staël returned upon being expelled from Paris by Napoleon for political intrigue. Madame de Staël was an important figure in Romantic circles of the late eighteenth and early nineteenth centuries. For a recent biography, see *Mistress to an Age*, by J. Christopher Herold (Indianapolis: Bobbs-Merrill Co., 1958). Ed.

surrounded by the deepest obscurity and contradiction. In our search for the new humanism was the issue of the survival and contemporary role of so-called "classical" humanism, that is, of classical Western humanism, of that humanism which the *Dictionnaire de l'Académie francaise*—obviously reflecting certain phenomena of the fourteenth and sixteenth centuries—defines as "a cultivation of spirit and soul, which comes from familiarity with classical literature, notably Greek and Roman"? Seen from that point of view, humanism, would be a kind of historical inheritance, which we would have to earn in order to possess: "an ideal of individual nobility, which one would like to see become that of the group." Now, even if one wanted to stand on this ground, the question would still have to be decided, whether this inheritance should be understood as a certain attitude determined by that tradition or as a particular philosophical doctrine, an anthropology. And here minds could and did divide clearly over the question: Which "classical" anthropology should be our concern? Platonic? Aristotelian? Stoic? But we could not, and most of us did not, wish to stand on that ground at all. The new humanism has nothing to do with ancient texts, some said. Others did not go so far, but they thought they must at least reckon seriously with the change in the picture of man and the world (especially in the natural sciences) which has appeared since the sixteenth century, and that they must therefore also take into account the existence of the many oriental "humanisms" which have entered our European consciousness since then, and which are in their own way genuine and respectable.

From this point of view, they said frankly that humanism consists in openly taking cognizance of other humanisms! But they preferred to define it negatively: It consists in the absence of all "exclusive" dogmas, in a fundamental spiritual openness toward all sides. It was described as man's understanding of himself, which continually changes throughout history. It was equated with freedom, therefore, or simply with man himself, or human life. Still others, trying to be more exactly and positively oriented toward real human life, claimed to recognize it simply in Communism or, more mildly, in the Co-operative movement. An especially bold definition stated, "Humanism is what we put into it," while another voice expressed itself more prudently, saying that it is "a critical reflection about man, of man about himself, about the human condition." It was apparently not possible, even in that group of widely trained and educated and well-intentioned men, to specify in common what we really wanted to discuss when we were talking about "humanism." Who was right? The man who declared quietly that his sleep was by no means disturbed by this lack of a definition of humanism? Or the other man, who thought he recognized the tragedy of the situation in this very indifference ("That is the drama," he said)?

And can we take it amiss that the theologians, although they followed the discussion with sincere and active interest, could follow only at a certain distance and in astonishment? But I should like to come back to this later. It seems to me to be appropriate to consider first some important examples, somewhat more concretely, of what came to light—or did not come to light—in Geneva with regard to humanism.

Humanism, we were carefully instructed, is supposed to be the prevalent conviction (which comes from the combination of Greek, Roman, Jewish, and Christian attitudes and traditions) of the value of the human person, in its unity of heart and head, knowledge and conscience. Its foundation is supposed to be faith in man, his decisive concern for the rights of the individual in the context of free institutions, his ideal of the world citizen, in the style of Leonardo, Erasmus, Leibniz, and Goethe. "Let us forget for a second, that we are Jews, Christians, free thinkers, Liberals, or Marxists." This humanism, therefore, is our common heritage. "Let each one of us be free to seek his origins at the Parthenon or on a mountain in Galilee." Two amplifications are decisively necessary for this humanism: that, following the example of the great Goethe, it integrate into itself the general hypotheses of contemporary natural science, and that it surrender its Mediterranean narrowness and enter into contact and exchange with the humanism of Islam, India, China, and Japan, and so become a "planetary humanism." To which one should add a third point: that it not remain the humanism of a privilege elite, that care should be taken, therefore, to make it possible for every man "to devote himself for a few moments each day to the best that is in him, to allow him, as the Indians would say, to discover again his own *âtman* in himself." The problem, or the problems, are difficult, René Grousset felt, but they are not insoluble.

A second meaning of humanism presented to us in Geneva was based on the view that the world is intelligible and man is perfectible, but it ended by being far less optimistic than the preceeding view. According to it, man is distinguished from animals in that he can never long exist under the same conditions of life. Cultural and civilizing progress results from his impulse toward change, and also much suffering results from this: separation between peoples, war. Not reason, but conscience alone—supported by an anthropology derived from careful observation, in the sense of Lévy-Brühl—can guarantee a certain righteousness. But that is precisely our occidental misery, that conscience and reason have gone their separate ways among us for centuries (most decisively since the sixteenth), and that includes faithfulness and progress, religion and metaphysics, and concretion and abstractions as well. The old, genuine Orient, which is our home too, is still aware of their unity. The Russians, even the Germans (German romanticism) are still aware of it. While, according to Paul Masson-Oursel, the French are the least "Indian" of peoples: "logicized," dried up by Cartesian rationalism—as though a people could live on the formula, "Liberty, Equality, Fraternity"! "We are almost dead, we poor Frenchmen, because we have forgotten that it is criminal to separate reason from life."

Well now, the third was quite a different customer: What is humanism? Answer: Man—free man; that is to say "whole" man, he the bearer of all values, he and only he the truly real being, who in the course of and as a consequence of his history transforms nature, the world, and with nature and the world, himself. What disturbs him, what impedes him? What alienates him from the way to his happiness, to the realization of his possibilities, and thus of himself? What isolates him as an individual and makes him into an impersonal mass? What separates man and woman, city and country, intellectual and physical work, class and class, man and things? One and only one thing: private ownership of the means of production! But history, that is, the social process of work, goes on, and its inner logic needs only to be understood and actually accepted. The whole man needs only to conceive of himself as the true subject of history and to get himself going, in order to become master of that deepest cause of all alienation, and thereby of that alienation itself, to overcome that separation collectively and individually. And that is just what he is in the act of doing victoriously in the form of the proletarian, the Communist, the Soviet man. "Communism," declared Henri Lefèbvre, in the words of Karl Marx, "is the return of man to himself as a social man, that is to say as an ultimately human man, a complete, conscious return with all the richness of previous development. Communism coincides with humanism."

After the Frenchmen, an Englishman: J. B. S. Haldane, he too a Communist, but a lyrical one, and obviously less mindful of Marxist orthodoxy than his French friend—tirelessly presenting himself as a "biologist," but possessed of an imposing intimacy with "classical" humanism. He was (not without signs of a certain scurrility) perhaps the most original figure at the symposium in Geneva. What is humanism? Being at home as a being endowed with reason in the sideritic and telluric universe, feeling oneself as matter, being proud of being an animal, a mammal—taking part without fear of pain and death in the conquest of our planet for life, which means for man, thinking, and, in fact, thinking biologically! For biology—not merely that of man, but also of plants and animals—not only recognizes nature, not only allows us and bids us to change it, it also leads from itself to morality, to the furthering of a society which gives each man the right to life. It also leads to revolutions, in which admittedly things do not happen without "a little intolerance." But even Protestantism was intolerant once. And certainly Communism will become tolerant one day. What is decisive is that each man understand himself in his personal inner world as a reflection of the larger outer world. If mystical experiences are possible, they cannot of themselves be articulated. If there exists a superhuman reason, its least trace cannot be noted by science, and anyway it does not seem to be concerned with our affairs. Whoever appeals to revelation needs to remember that the sayings of the prophets were as a rule not fulfilled. If there exists a hierarchy in nature, a theology of history, a special vocation of man, all that is in any case not demonstrable and not even necessary for us to know. If humanity does and must combat the other elements of the universe, as bacteria do too, it would be a lack of humility to consider this struggle—and the struggle for a classless society—as the meaning of the universe. Likewise, even Existentialism is to be rejected because of its exaggerated emphasis on individual consciousness.

And now finally the voice of German philosophy: What is man? He is more than what he can know of himself. He is not only an object; he is free. He is free in that he has been given to himself, in the transcendence, which he can neither take for himself, nor give to himself, but which he will also never lack, although of course he can never be sure of it. He exists when he decides, each for himself, for his own being. Thus, he is never complete, always imperfect and imperfectible, always merely on the way into an unknown future. But just because of this he is never condemned to despair either. He is in danger of losing himself in this technical age, of becoming a cog in a machine. The task, therefore, is to put technical science in the inner and outward service of human life. Even politics has become unscrupulous, mechanical, fateful. Here we must lead the superior might of freedom and order into battle against despotism and anarchy. The old "Western world," the God of a commonly held faith, man as a universally valid ideal have all been lost to us today. What we need is a new doctrinal basis, a new entity of concepts and symbols in the place of the Catholicism which has become unacceptable to most of us. We are looking for this. We have not found it yet, however. In the meantime, humanity as a

---

whole is threatened. Everywhere there is destruction. Everywhere things are coming to a halt. But that is precisely our special fortune today. And if we do not know anything, at least we do not know that we are really lost either. The very creditable tradition of the Occident remains for us. Let us nurture it and unite it realistically—but without becoming antihuman—with the social demands of the present and the spiritual traditions of the East.

The individual who corresponds to this picture has known at all times how to make himself heard, from Isaiah through Socrates and Jesus up to Spinoza and Kant, and he will do it in the future too. He will stress his free and yet responsible humanity, which withdraws from fiction and falsehood, which still exists in communication with others, and which is still founded upon its transcendence. Philosophy can only call man's attention to it. It can only teach him to think in an orderly manner. It can only lead him toward freedom from all absolutes. Insofar as it does that, it may be compared with the prayer of those who believe in revelation. But there remains a continual temptation for human life. We follow a star which will lead us only by virtue of the lucidity of our own decision. We affirm life, as though we had help out of the depths, which at least signifies the comfort of being allowed to seek what we have desired, not in vain, but in some relation to being. This is the philosophy of existence which Karl Jaspers laid before us in Geneva.

I shall break off my report, which is meant only to offer examples, and shall skip over, among others, the two theological lectures which were delivered in Geneva by the French Dominican Father Maydieu and myself. Let it be expressly said that even we were listened to in a friendly, attentive, and respectable manner. I should like to indicate, in the form of some free reminiscences and reflections, some of the things which may be said from a theological standpoint to what I have just been describing.

1. My Catholic colleague and I were in striking agreement in that, along with more important things, we did *not* feel we had to place the conceptions presented by the other participants alongside of or opposite to a "*Christian* humanism." I say "striking" because I consider it probable that some other representatives of the Roman Catholic Church would have done precisely what Father Maydieu did not do. "Christian Humanism" is an awkward tool; this has been revealed in every attempt to use it. The attempt should be avoided, if only for the fact that all words ending in "ism" are inappropriate in serious theological language. They speak of principles and systems. They proclaim a point of view or a moral philosophy. They announce the existence of a Front or a Party. The gospel, however, is neither a principle, nor a system, nor a point of view, nor a moral philosophy. It is spirit and life, a good message of God's presence and work in Jesus Christ. It does not form some Front or Party either, not even for the sake of a certain conception of man. It forms congregations, and these exist for service among all men.

The question of man, of course, is also central in the gospel. But what is to be said from the gospel *about* man, for man (and *against* man too) begins where the different humanisms leave off; or it leaves off where they begin. One can understand them all from the gospel, and affirm them and hold them to be valid for a good part of the way. My Catholic neighbor in Geneva even struck up a paean to the "creative man," which I could not have done so beautifully. But from the gospel, one must finally contradict all humanisms, just because they are humanisms, abstract programs. Theology does not compete with them. It has nothing equivalent or similar with which to confront them. It can certainly take up the concept of humanism, although it was originally formed without theology, in fact in opposition to theology. But theology can take no responsibility for the definition of humanism. It cannot conceal the fact that it would not be surprised if its definition should ultimately prove to be unfeasible. It tastes at the same time of both a little godlessness and a little idolatry. I myself spoke in Geneva about "the humanism of God" in a conscious inversion of the historical and abstract sense of this concept, which should not, however, be thought of as a humanity originated and made to work by man, but as God's friendliness to man as the source and norm of all human rights and all human dignity.

2. Father Maydieu did not for a moment hide the light of his Catholic, Thomistic thought under a bushel, and I think that I spoke just as unsecretively there as a Protestant theologian. The audience certainly noticed the difference, and the "more wicked" of the two Marxists participating did not fail to call attention to it explicitly, not without malice. It seemed as though the Protestant, at least as a humanly attractive proponent of a "thought which goes to the limit," had found relatively greater grace in his eyes. But what was really remarkable in Geneva was not the difference of the confessional positions, but the unity of the Christian, the theological positions in the face of all the others, a unity which was, in spite of all, not to be mistaken this time. It was felt very clearly, especially by Karl Jaspers, who was able to scent the same horrible claim to the absolute in both the Catholic and me—no matter how we might explain ourselves and distinguish shades of meaning—of what he called a "religion of revelation." I shall come back to these things later.

In any case, it could not be overlooked that in fact in the midst of all the gaping contradictions of the different human-isms, the Christian view of the problem—which of course did not prevail—had at least the advantage of a certain unity, despite all inner differences. It was, in a remarkable way, also decisively greater than that which the two representatives of Marxism presented there. If Father Maydieu thought more from below upwards, and I from above downwards, we met together in the thesis that the problem of so-called "human-ism" has been fundamentally answered in Jesus Christ and that all "new humanism" can only consist in man's again recognizing in the mirror of this one person simultaneously the face of the one true God, and the face of the one true man.

The proceedings reminded me of the experience of the Amsterdam Assembly in 1948. The Christian footing is cer-tainly also a very human footing, but it is of such a nature—in contrast to that of the United Nations, UNESCO, or such free intellectual congresses as this one—that on it persons can not only speak and listen to one another humanly (although com-ing from widely divergent standpoints, as is well known) but can find and work out communication precisely in the ultim-ate questions, and can say the same things in different words to a large extent. Not because Christians and theologians might be especially excellent and clever, or even just especially irenic creatures, but because on this footing there are a free-dom and a bond which overcome human contradictions and which cannot possibly remain invisible.

3. I assume that my report of those five examples has given some impression of the unique amphibole, the relativity and ambiguity of feelings and views, in which the conference in Geneva was tossed back and forth in those ten days. On the one hand, there was optimism, but it was a rather tired and

sickly optimism, neither convinced nor convincing, always placing itself and its proponents in question, directly or indirectly. On the other hand, there was the position of *pessimism*, but a particularly respectable, spiritually wealthy and elegant—one might almost say amusing—pessimism, which clearly did not take itself seriously. Often enough, both of these tendencies, each equally fragile, could be seen in one and the same person, in one and the same lecture or vote! How rare were the moments in which the impression of a subjectively honest joy was made, in at least calling upon the much-named "faith in man," as happened for example, so far as I could see, now and then in the votes of the Communist Henri Lefèbvre! And how rare, on the other hand, were there any groans—as for example those of Paul Masson-Oursel over his rationalistic Frenchmen—which at least seemed to come from the depths of the heart! And how are we to take it seriously when Karl Jaspers—to whom I do not wish to stand too close in saying this—at first assured us that the contemporary world had become an infernal chaos, only to comfort us later by saying that of course we could not know for sure that man is really lost? I ask: Has real man, contemporary man, come into this picture at all? Would he not actually be easier to see in any diary of the past twenty years without philosophical trimmings? But could he be seen at all when the problem of guilt was not so much as touched on in those ten days, and where the problem of death was only barely touched, and that in a somewhat arrogant fashion? And how could man be seen, on the other hand, where no one could speak out of a genuine, comforting certainty and hope? The Marxist certainty and hope of Henri Lefèbvre was surely too convulsive, too fanatical, too uncomforting to be named as an exception. Oddly enough, he was the one who described the

127

effect on him of my lecture with the following words: "I felt pass through me a sort of religious tremor, the feeling of sin. Repent! I felt that mixture of terror and hope which has been, for some ten centuries, the basis of religious emotion." Precisely, for some ten centuries—to be more exact, for nineteen hundred years!

Naturally Henri Lefèbvre had no idea of becoming "converted." But he seemed to have seen the problem for a moment, at least from a distance, the problem which burdened the conference in Geneva and which also leads all similar discussions in our time into a dead-end: How can we speak constructively about what is meant by the label "humanism," about real contemporary man and his future if we do not know and do not *want* to know that man is in fact lost and also in fact saved, if one does not know and does not want to know the true horror and the true hope of our situation? The true man for all time is the lost and rescued man who is seen in the mirror of Jesus Christ. How can a conversation about this man have even a meaningful beginning if one shies like a scared horse at the Christian confession and its word of God's judgment and grace, if one has nothing more to set against it than the sentimental lament over its "exclusiveness"? How can there be even a beginning if one always flees into the ambiguities of that lukewarm religion of semi-earnestness and semi-consolation, found in the middle, or rather, *under* the middle in some obscure depth, away from the horror which must really be feared and the hope which may be grasped with confidence?

4. Yes, the "exclusiveness" of the Christian proclamation and theology! That theme played a considerable role in Geneva, especially in the position of my honored Basel

colleague Jaspers,[1] but clearly also in the wider circle of the public there present. No Thomistic mildness or broadmindedness on the part of Father Maydieu was of any help here, and neither was any "Basel wit," as it was called, on my part. Evidently there were not a few who, in spite of everything, suffered an anxiety which they could not get rid of, that then and there the fate of Servetus awaited them, simply because at the decisive point neither of us could deny where we stood, but for better or worse had to make our confession of faith.

At this point I cannot suppress a general reflection: Some two hundred and fifty years ago, it was the theologians, not all but many of them, who stood in anxious fear before the critique of the philosophers, the historians, the natural scientists, and to some extent all the rest of the liberal and skeptical scholarly profession. They had a real inferiority complex before them, even if it was more or less hidden. This anxiety on the part of theologians has done a great deal of damage these past two hundred and fifty years. But now for the first time, I am clearly confronted by the same phenomenon, a sort of inferiority complex, again not in all, but in quite a few, and this time on the other side. With the exception of the Englishman Haldane, a true son of the Enlightenment, they met us with hardly a noteworthy, relevant criticism of our statements. In this respect, the eighteenth and nineteenth centuries are clearly things of the past for them, But from us they fear I know not what condemnation, excommunication, or damnation for their unbelief. They absolutely refused to observe the fact that neither Father Maydieu nor I had so much as suggested that sort of thing in our lectures. They also

[1] Jaspers and Barth were both professors at the University of Basel, Switzerland, when this was written. Ed.

refused to take us seriously when we said to them that a Christian and a theologian must of necessity be far more concerned with his own unbelief than with that of other people, with whom he can only know himself to stand in all too strong a solidarity in this area. All they would say to us again and again was that the "claim of absoluteness" of the "religion of revelation" was a horrible, dangerous, and unbearable thing.

Now just which page is it that has begun to turn here? Are matters to proceed between us theologians and the others in the future as in that scene in Mozart's *The Magic Flute*, in which the bird-catcher Papageno and the Moor Monostatos flee from each other with the wild cry, "Surely t'is the devil, he! Have mercy, oh protect poor me! Oh! Oh! Oh!"? Or might it not be high time, as the basis for all further contact, to free ourselves on both sides and fundamentally from all fear? In Geneva, however, we had not come so far—and this was true primarily of the worthy representatives of modern liberalism. And the worst of it was that we theologians were looked on as standing, in this respect, all too near, of all people, the *Communists*! I quote word for word the contribution of one of those in the discussion: "Since the beginning, I have felt myself caught between two jaws: on the one hand, Professor Barth and the Reverend Father Maydieu say to us: 'Be converted and all will be simple!' On the other hand, Henri Lefèbvre answers, 'Imitate the *homo sovietcus*, or at least consult the secretary of the nearest party cell and likewise all will be in good order!' I find myself caught in a dilemma in which I recognize two religious faiths—which, at least in some respects, have this in common, that they are prolongations of the messianism of Israel."

It must indeed be terrible to feel oneself so caught with the

Last Judgment and perhaps the funeral pyre of Servetus threatening on one side and the dictatorship of the proletariat and exile to Siberia threatening on the other, especially for one who wants to be what this speaker explicitly called himself: a humanist whose honor lies in being an "agnostic," i.e., a man who has decided not to decide and to accept no definite responsibility. The spirit of flight from decision and responsibility, properly clothed as "agnosticism," was perhaps one of the secrets of a certain stagnation which beset us in Geneva as we discussed the problem of "humanism" and "the new humanism." It is clear that neither the Dominican nor I could very well take part in this flight and just because of this—*ceteris imparibus*—must have looked a bit similar to the Communists. For that which is called the "exclusiveness" of the Christian proclamation and Christian theology, when looked at in its own terms, consists in this—and this is what it may have in common with Communism, in a formal sense— that it summons men to decision and responsibility, to faith and obedience. From case to case, but also fundamentally and permanently, it calls men to a binding decision and responsibility, to a freedom which is the highest and truest freedom, since it is that of the free man who knows himself in all serenity to be a man who is called, ordered, and obligated.

The "messianism of Israel" is not the meaning and basis of this freedom. God preserve us also from this -ism! I do not know whether it is one of the roots of Communism. It could be. The meaning and basis of the Christian message and theology, in any case, is, to say it once more, beyond all principles and systems, all world-views and morality, not messianism, but rather the Messiah, the Christ of Israel. If the confession of Him as the sole Savior of the world is to be called "exclusiveness," then we must let this charge stand.

———

No one is forced to make this confession. But there is no sense in giving oneself out as a Christian if for any reason one does not think one has the freedom to make this confession. In truth, it is basically a confession which is "inclusive," which bears upon, and is open to, every man.

The Christian Church does not speak from out of heaven. It speaks on earth and in an earthly way. In the alloted place assigned to it, however, it has this and only this to say to the problem of humanism, today as always, this in its exclusiveness and inclusiveness, this which includes all else, and this as the basis for all else: *Et incarnatus est de Spiritu Sanctu ex Maria virgine et homo factus est*. Over against all other humanisms, the Church points to this as the light which will burn the longest.

INDEX

Routledge Classics
Get inside a great mind

Between Man and Man
Martin Buber

'Martin Buber is practically the only religious writer a non-religious person could take seriously today.'
Kenneth Rexroth

Martin Buber believed that the deepest reality of human life lies in the relationship between one being and another. *Between Man and Man* is the classic book in which he puts this belief into practice, applying it to the concrete problems of contemporary society. Including some of his most famous writings, such as the masterful 'What is Man?', this enlightening work challenges each reader to reassess their encounter with the world that surrounds them.

Hb: 0–415–27826–0   Pb: 0–415–27827–9

The Way of Man
According to the teachings of Hasidism
Martin Buber

'Like no other author, Buber has enriched the world literature with a genuine treasure.'
Hermann Hesse

In this short and remarkable book Martin Buber presents the essential teachings of Hasidism, the mystical Jewish movement which swept through Eastern Europe in the eighteenth and nineteenth centuries. Told through stories of imagination and spirit, together with his own unique insights, Buber offers us a way of understanding ourselves and our place in a spiritual world. Challenging us to recognize our own potential and to reach our true goal, *The Way of Man* is a life-enhancing book.

Hb: 0–415–27828–7   Pb: 0–415–27829–5

For these and other classic titles from Routledge, visit
www.routledgeclassics.com

Routledge Classics
Get inside a great mind

Letter to a Priest
Simone Weil

'The best spiritual writer of this century.'
André Gide

Regarded by Susan Sontag as 'one of the most uncompromising and troubling witnesses to the modern travail of the spirit', Weil grips the moral imagination as few others before or since. Written at a time when those who knew her considered her to be 'like a soul in torment whose thinking had all the signs of a deep inner conflict', it contains thirty-five powerful expressions of opinion on matters concerning Catholic faith, dogma and institutions. Vehement and controversial, yet eloquent and moving, it is essential reading for anyone who has questions about faith and belief.

Hb: 0–415–26766–8   Pb: 0–415–26767–6

Gravity and Grace
Simone Weil

'The light Simone shines makes everything seem, at once, reassuringly recognizable and so luminous as to be heavenly.'
Malcolm Muggeridge

Gravity and Grace was the first-ever publication by the remarkable thinker and activist, Simone Weil. Gustave Thibon, to whom she had entrusted her notebooks before her untimely death, compiled, in one remarkable volume, a compendium of her writings that has become a source of spiritual guidance and wisdom for countless individuals. This is a book that no one with a serious interest in the spiritual life can afford to be without.

Hb: 0–415–29000–7   Pb: 0–415–29001–5

For these and other classic titles from Routledge, visit
www.routledgeclassics.com

Routledge Classics
Get inside a great mind

Mysticism: Christian and Buddhist
D. T. Suzuki

'Read the books of D. T. Suzuki.'
Jack Kerouac

If the Western world knows anything about Zen Buddhism, it is down to the efforts of one remarkable man, D. T. Suzuki. The 27-year-old Japanese scholar first visited the West in 1897, and over the course of the next seventy years became the world's leading authority on Zen. His radical and penetrating insights earned him many disciples, from Carl Gustav Jung to Allen Ginsberg, and from Thomas Merton to John Cage. In *Mysticism: Christian and Buddhist* Suzuki compares the teachings of the great Christian mystic Meister Eckhart with the spiritual wisdom of Shin and Zen Buddhism.

Hb: 0–415–28585–2   Pb: 0–415–28586–0

Myth and Meaning
Claude Lévi-Strauss

'Some thinkers are influential, a few create schools, a very few characterize a period . . . it is possible that just as we speak of the age of Aquinas or of Goethe, later ages will speak of our time as the age of Claude Lévi-Strauss . . . he is a maker of the modern mind.'
Professor James Redfield, University of Chicago

In addresses written for a wide general audience, one of the twentieth century's most prominent thinkers, Claude Lévi-Strauss, here offers the insights of a lifetime on the crucial questions of human existence. Responding to questions as varied as 'Can there be meaning in chaos?', 'What can science learn from myth?' and 'What is structuralism?', Lévi-Strauss presents, in clear, precise language, essential guidance for those who want to learn more about the potential of the human mind.

Hb: 0–415–25548–1   Pb: 0–415–25394–2

For these and other classic titles from Routledge, visit
www.routledgeclassics.com